Fresh Vegetables and Herbs from Your Garden

Fresh Vegetables and Herbs from Your Garden

Percy Thrower VMH

HAMLYN
London · New York · Sydney · Toronto

Acknowledgements

Line drawings by Ron Hayward

Colour photographs by *Amateur Gardening*,
Valerie Finnis, Harry Smith, The Hamlyn Publishing Group Limited

Frontispiece The author removing some foliage
from his tomato plants so that more light can
reach the fruits

First Published in 1974 by
The Hamlyn Publishing Group Limited
London · New York · Sydney · Toronto
Astronaut House, Feltham, Middlesex, England
Fourth impression 1976

© Percy Thrower and the Hamlyn Publishing
Group Limited 1974

ISBN 0 600 33505 4

Distributed in the USA by Crescent Books

Printed in England by Chapel River Press
Andover, Hampshire
Filmset in England by Trade Spools
Frome, Somerset

Contents

Why Grow Vegetables?

In all but the smallest gardens I feel an area should be set aside for vegetables. Vegetable growing is fun, and it is satisfying to be able to eat the results of your labours. More than this, it really is a fact that many vegetables freshly harvested have a flavour which is unknown in shop bought ones.

Probably more important to most people at the moment is the question of economy and when the family numbers, say, four or more there can be quite a big saving in the greengrocer's bill if a reasonable area is available in the garden for vegetables. Of course, it is important to consider vegetable growing objectively and to work out a range of crops which takes economics into account. This means concentrating on growing those which are always more expensive and aiming at maturing crops at a time when they are scarce and, once again, particularly expensive.

Another important objective should be to produce the family's favourites and not only the stock crops like potatoes, cabbages and cauliflowers which readily spring to mind. Some vegetables are easier to grow than others and I suggest that a beginner would do well to try first such crops as lettuce, radish, beetroot, brussels sprouts and cabbage. Peas are fairly easy and runner beans also if they are given all the moisture they need. And for a couple of unusual vegetables, which are particularly good for winter salads, do try chicory and endive.

In order to get maximum value from the area available much will depend on making full use of the ground and cropping it to capacity and here it is most important to master the techniques of successional sowing, intercropping and catch cropping.

Successional sowing is applicable to most crops, especially the salad ones, and simply means sowing a little and often to produce an amount of each vegetable which can be coped with instead of an impossible glut. In order to get the best possible results from this it really is worthwhile to invest in some form of protection to allow seed to be sown earlier than outside conditions permit. A greenhouse is the ideal, particularly if combined with some garden frames, but even the relatively inexpensive plastic cloches can make a lot of difference to the sowing times as well as providing protection for newly planted seedlings or for crops which mature later in the year.

Catch cropping and intercropping consist of sowing quick maturing crops in the periods when the ground is not occupied by main crops and in growing salad crops between others which remain in the ground for much longer periods. Learning to make the maximum use of the area available for cropping is essential if you are to recoup all the effort you have put into the cultivation as well as making full use of the manure and fertilizer that have been used on the ground.

Even a small area can be used to grow a wide range of vegetables, particularly if cloches are available to hasten the cropping period

The possibility of growing some vegetables in pots and tubs is also well worth considering as these have a special place in the patio or paved garden or even on balconies. Certain vegetables grow extremely well in this way and produce reasonable size crops, so if garden space is in short supply then I suggest that you try runner beans, french beans, the Courgette variety of bush marrow, early potatoes, tomatoes and even a few roots of rhubarb. Use large size pots or other suitable containers and John Innes No. 3 potting compost or a similar compost as the growing medium. It is essential to pay strict attention to the watering and feeding of plants grown in this way.

Herbs, too, should have a place in every garden. Fresh parsley, mint, sage and thyme, to mention only the most popular, make a tremendous difference to culinary dishes and these, together with the others which can be easily grown, are described later in the book. Once again, herbs are plants which thrive in containers and are, therefore, very useful for growing in the small garden or, indeed, for a flat dweller with access only to a window box or at best a balcony.

Planning the Garden

For many people who are growing vegetables for the first time, the main problem is where to site the vegetable garden. In my opinion it wants to be away from the house but it must be in an open light position and not tucked away under trees or shaded by buildings. When selecting the position remember that the three fundamental requirements for good results are sun, good soil and sufficient water.

I prefer to screen the vegetable garden from the windows of the house. To do this you can plant either a productive screen such as cordon-trained fruit trees trained at an angle of 45 degrees – this is what I have at the top of my garden – or a purely ornamental hedge. For this there is a plentiful choice: beech, *Cupressocyparis leylandii*, *Chamaecyparis lawsoniana*, *Lonicera nitida*, escallonia or forsythia if you want a flowering hedge, or a very attractive subject is the golden variegated *Thuja zebrina*.

Soil Most soils can be adapted to grow the majority of vegetables. What we would all like – but usually have not got – is a fibrous medium loam with plenty of body in it. What in reality we are most likely to have to cope with is a soil which is either too light and free draining or too heavy and water retentive for the needs of most plants. Fortunately there is a fairly easy way of overcoming both these faults and this is by good cultivation – mixing in plenty of organic matter such as manure, garden compost or peat, liming to improve texture and provide the necessary calcium and the addition of fertilizers to provide the essential plant foods.

Some plants do best in, and in fact prefer, acid soil; others will only grow well in an alkaline soil (in Britain this is a soil containing free lime), so it is a good idea to find out which kind you have. This is simply done with a soil testing kit which can be obtained quite cheaply from garden centres and garden sundriesmen. If the soil is shown to be very acid, or the plants you are putting in prefer an alkaline soil, then a dressing of lime should be applied about a couple of months after digging. The best form to use is hydrated lime and the amount to apply will depend on the existing degree of acidity – 3 oz. to the sq. yd. would be an average dressing. Most vegetables grow well in a slightly acid to neutral soil, potatoes need a rather more acid soil while brassicas, peas and beans prefer an alkaline soil.

Size Any plot, however tiny, is capable of providing some of the vegetable needs of the family even if it is only used to produce early salads. To give you some guidance on size, a plot 30 ft. × 10 ft. would be large enough to grow lettuce, radish, carrots, beetroot, runner beans and peas for the summer, and for winter cropping celery, cabbage, brussels sprouts, sprouting broccoli and leeks. On the other hand, an area of 90 ft. × 30 ft. (the standard allotment size in Britain) can provide suffi-

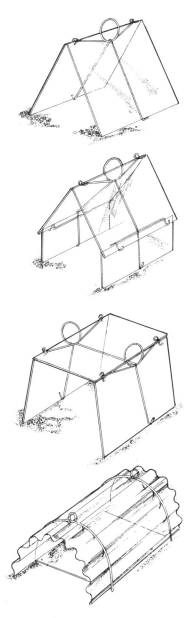

Types of cloches

Some form of protection, such as a greenhouse, frames or cloches, is helpful in the production of early crops

cient vegetables, with the exception of main crop potatoes, to keep a family of four supplied throughout the year. I do not grow main crop potatoes as these are heavy on space and subject to a lot of diseases, but it is worth growing some rows of an early variety.

Whatever the size of the area good planning and the use of planting systems such as catch cropping and intercropping (see page 13) will ensure that the best possible use is made of the ground. Some crops are also more economical than others and give greater returns for the space required to grow them and here I am thinking particularly of runner beans and brussels sprouts, and also broad beans and peas, which are quick maturing. The important point with quick maturing crops is to follow one with another, filling up the ground as soon as you have cleared the proceeding crop.

On page 12 there are plans showing suggested planting schemes for two vegetable plots, one large and one small. These are based on my preferences and, of course, they can be altered to fall in line with the tastes of your family. I do consider that it is most important that you establish a cropping plan before you start the winter cultivations. You will then be able to mark the areas which are to receive additions of organic matter. Similarly, it is possible to establish the areas which are to receive dressings of fertilizer and lime. See crop rotation.

Early crops I would like to put in a word here about the value of early crops, that is timing the cultivations to bring certain vegetables to maturity before they are available in the shops or when they are at their most expensive. To do this it will be necessary to have some form of ancillary equipment such as cloches, frames or a greenhouse, to provide protection early in the year. Plastic cloches are relatively inexpensive but with their help it is possible to advance the sowing dates of a number of crops and to have fresh salads early in the season as well as carrots, peas, onions and even broad beans from a fortnight to four weeks sooner than they would normally appear in the shops.

Crop rotation Where space allows, vegetables should always be grown in a rotation system so that no crop is planted on the same piece of ground two years running. There are two main reasons for this. First, different crops take different amounts of foodstuffs from the soil. For example, cabbages, brussels sprouts, broccoli and cauliflower (all known as brassica crops) take large quantities of nitrogen from the soil, whereas peas and beans are capable of absorbing nitrogen from the air and therefore leave a surplus in the soil for other crops. By making sure that crops are grown in different plots each year, the soil is not depleted so rapidly of plant foods. The second reason for rotating crops is that it discourages the build up of pests and diseases to damaging proportions. For instance, club root is a major disease in many gardens in Britain and it can only be eradicated if brassica crops are kept off the affected area for three or four seasons. Other troubles controlled by rotation include potato-root eelworm and white rot of onions.

A common method of rotational cropping is to divide the ground into three approximately equal sections. The first year one section is used to grow potatoes and root crops (plot 1), another to grow leeks, onions, peas, beans, celery and lettuces (plot 2) and the third to grow cauliflowers, cabbages, brussels sprouts and other green crops (plot 3). Then the next year the groups are shifted round – the potatoes and root crops go to

Left plot (10 ft. × 30 ft.)

10 ft.
onions
runner beans *(followed by spring cabbage)* / lettuce and radish as intercrops
carrots *(followed by endive)*
peas *(followed by winter spinach)* / lettuce as an intercrop
beetroot
celery / lettuce and radish as catch crops
leeks
broccoli and cauliflower / spring onions and lettuce as intercrops
brussels sprouts / summer spinach as an intercrop

(height: 30 ft.)

Right plot (30 ft. × 90 ft.)

cucumber	tomatoes / herbs	rhubarb	compost heap

PATH

early potatoes *(followed by spring cabbage)*

beetroot	carrots
parsnips	seakale
swedes	chicory

PATH

runner beans / lettuce as an intercrop	marrows
broad beans	spinach
peas / lettuce and radish as intercrops	cabbage
french beans / spring onions as an intercrop	broccoli – sprouting and heading
celery / lettuce and radish as catch crops	cauliflower
onions	brussels sprouts
leeks	
endive	

(height: 90 ft.)

2 ft.

plot 2, the peas and beans to plot 3 and the cabbages to plot 1. A similar change is made in the third year, and in the fourth year the crops are back to their starting quarters and the whole cycle can then be repeated. This system also ensures that manure or compost, fertilizer and lime are only provided for the various crops when they are required and in this way you will get full value for money spent on fertilizers. The diagram of crop rotation shows the stages when the fertilizers are applied.

First Year

PLOT ONE—APPLY GENERAL FERTILIZER

Beetroot · Carrots · Kohl-rabi · Potatoes · Salsify · Scorzonera · Turnips · Swedes · Celeriac · Parsnips

PLOT TWO—DIG IN COMPOST OR MANURE

Beans · Peas · Leeks · Lettuces · Onions · Shallots · Celery · Endive · Radish

PLOT THREE—APPLY LIME IF NECESSARY, FERTILIZER BEFORE SOWING

Cabbage · Brussels sprouts · Broccoli · Cauliflower · Kale · Savoy · Spinach

Second Year

PLOT THREE

PLOT ONE

PLOT TWO

Third Year

PLOT TWO

PLOT THREE

PLOT ONE

Fourth Year
The cycle begins again

This diagram is meant for your guidance only. On a small area it is practically impossible to employ a rotational system and even in a larger area you may not wish to grow all the crops mentioned. If you are planning to grow some of the permanent crops such as asparagus, rhubarb and herbs, these will fall outside the rotational system and should be sited at one end of the vegetable garden where they can be left undisturbed.

Catch cropping and intercropping As you become more experienced in vegetable growing, it is possible to increase crop yields and therefore gain far more from the available space. This is done by catch cropping and intercropping. For certain vegetables the ground has to be prepared some time in advance of when it will be needed and catch cropping consists of growing a quick-maturing crop in this reserved area of ground and getting it harvested before the main crop is ready for sowing or planting. Lettuce, summer spinach, radishes and spring onions are some of the crops you can use for this purpose. Lettuce and radishes can be grown, for instance, between the trenches prepared for celery, provided they are off the ground before the celery needs earthing up, or they can be grown on a plot prepared for winter greens.

Another method of saving space is by intercropping – growing quick-maturing vegetables between others which remain in the ground for much longer periods or which are planted wide apart to prevent one row shading the next. In the space between the rows it is possible to grow a crop which will be off the ground before the main crop has grown enough to need all its allotted space. For example, brussels sprouts are planted 3 ft. apart so I use that space in the early stages for growing radishes or lettuce and, similarly, where I am growing peas and beans that need to be 2 ft. or more apart, I again make use of that area.

Far left Planting scheme for an area of 10 by 30 ft.
Left Planting scheme for an area of 30 by 90 ft.

The Essential Preliminaries

The best time to start making a vegetable garden is in the autumn for it is then that you must plan for the year ahead. To grow good vegetables you must have well-cultivated soil and I feel strongly that at least one-third of the vegetable garden should have manure, garden compost, peat or other humus-forming material dug into it once a year. But do remember that carrots and parsnips should not be grown in recently manured soil as this causes the roots to fork. A soil which is properly cultivated and contains plenty of organic matter holds more soil water, and retains plant food instead of allowing it to be washed out.

Vegetables, on the whole, grow quickly and anything which checks growth, such as shortage of water or lack of food, results in poorly developed crops. This shows up as small stringy roots on root crops, running to seed in celery, small and yellow leaves on brassicas and similar crops and poor quality pods produced in inadequate numbers on peas and beans. So, the soil must be well cultivated, well manured and well fed, it must be kept sufficiently moist and – very important – free of weeds.

Drainage At an early stage it is essential to determine if the natural drainage is sufficient to cope with all likely weather conditions. If there is any reason to doubt this, it is a good idea to dig 2- to 3-ft. deep holes in several places in the garden and then see if these hold water after heavy rain. Land which is low lying or very heavy is liable to suffer from bad drainage and the waterlogging associated with this will result in the roots of plants dying and often the complete loss of the plants. Three-

Left Hoeing is an important cultural operation
Below Two drainage systems, one using land-drain pipes, the other consisting of a trench containing rubble

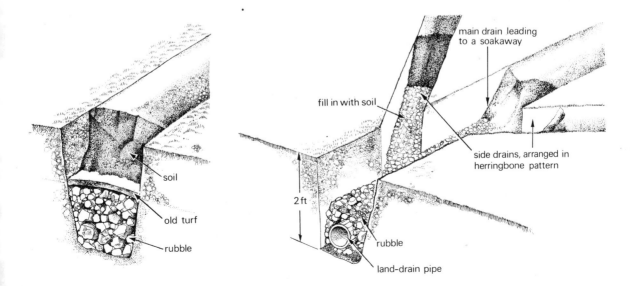

soil

old turf

rubble

main drain leading to a soakaway

fill in with soil

side drains, arranged in herringbone pattern

2 ft

rubble

land-drain pipe

inch-diameter land-drain pipes, put 2 ft. underground and leading to a suitable pit or soak-away placed at the lowest point on the land, provide the best remedy but a trench, partly filled with rubble, covered first with a layer of turf and then with soil to surface level, is usually quite effective.

Soil preparation The most common soil type in Britain is clay, which can be difficult to work. But there are few better growing mediums than a clay soil which has been cultivated and improved over a matter of years. With such soils drainage is of paramount importance for in the nature of things they are extremely retentive of moisture, the individual soil particles being very small indeed. The humus-forming materials – manure, garden compost and other forms of organic matter – break up the close-packed soil particles and so allow excess moisture to drain freely to lower levels. One of the key factors in the successful mastery of clay soils is timing one's cultivations correctly. Working them in wet weather, for instance, is folly of the worst kind, for the compaction which results can do enormous harm. So never attempt to dig such soils when they are so wet that the particles pick up on your boots. On the other hand, digging during good weather in autumn so that the surface can be left rough is ideal. The frost, snow and rain will then break down the large lumps and make the task of seed bed preparation in spring a comparatively easy chore. If farmyard manure, garden compost or leaves are dug in at this time make sure that they are well rotted. Spent mushroom compost and spent hops are both good for this purpose, and so are fish manure, sewage sludge and seaweed manure.

If your soil is light and quick draining, the organic matter is best applied only about a month to six weeks before seed sowing. If it is applied too early, the food will be washed down into the lower levels of the soil and so will be unavailable to the vegetables when they need it.

Digging is just about the heaviest job in the garden and if you have a plot of a reasonable size – say, the standard allotment area – it would probably be worthwhile hiring a powered cultivator, which will make the task much easier.

However, whether you dig with a spade, fork or by mechanical means do make sure that the soil is well broken up – at least to a depth of 10 in. (or the height of a spade's blade) – and if organic matter is to be incorporated, spread it on the surface and then turn it under during the digging process.

Garden compost Large quantities of organic matter are used in improving soil texture and with farmyard manure so difficult to obtain nowadays it is important that all waste green material, including vegetable refuse, should be saved for composting.

The compost heap can be made up from a range of waste materials including grass and hedge clippings, leaves, vegetable and fruit refuse. I always say that if it grows, it can be composted, with the exception of diseased or pest-ridden material and weeds which have gone to seed or have thick roots such as bind weed or couch grass. Such material is better burned and the ashes sprinkled on the compost heap. Build the heap about 3 ft. high and 3 ft. through and it is a good idea to surround it with plastic-covered wire netting to keep it tidy. To encourage and increase the rate of decay use an accelerator, such as Nitro-chalk, sulphate of ammonia or one of the proprietary products made for this purpose, dusting it lightly over each 9-in. layer of refuse. If sulphate of ammonia is used as an accelerator, then it should be alternated between the layers with hydrated lime. While building the heap, wet thoroughly any material which appears dry.

After about a month turn the heap, bringing the inner portions to the outside and turning the outside in, and whilst turning water any dry parts. Once the heap has decayed to a brown mass in which the original components are not discernible, it can be used like manure.

Chemical fertilizers While the humus-forming materials I have mentioned do much to improve the physical condition of the soil, they are very unreliable sources of food and with some crops it is essential to apply concentrated fertilizers supplying one or more of the three main plant foods – nitrogen, phosphorus and potassium.

As an aid in deciding which fertilizers to use, it is helpful to know something of the effect of each of these chemicals.

Nitrogen, sometimes expressed as 'N' on fertilizer bags, encourages good colour and vigour of growth of leaves and so is especially valuable for crops such as spinach, lettuce and cabbage. A deficiency will be shown up by small, pale or, sometimes, bluish foliage and stunted plants.

Phosphorus may be referred to by manufacturers as phosphate or indicated simply by the letter 'P'. This chemical is beneficial to root vegetables and the formation of roots in general, including those of newly planted seeds. It also helps in the production of flowers and in the ripening of fruits and seeds. Most deficiency symptoms are very similar to those of nitrogen but poor, stunted root systems also indicate a lack of this chemical.

Potassium, potash or 'K', has a range of effects – helping to produce disease resistance, strong stems and generally improving the size and colour of fruits and root vegetables. A deficiency is indicated by stunted growth, weak stems and the older leaves turning yellow around the edges.

However, although one can describe the individual effect of each of these chemicals it is important to realize that the results of their actions are closely linked and so it is essential to achieve the correct balance between them when adding them to the soil. For this reason, for most purposes I would choose a general garden fertilizer which shows an analysis of 7 to 8 per cent. nitrogen, 5 to 6 per cent. phosphate and the same of potash. The chemical constituents of all proprietary fertilizers are shown on the outside of the bag.

Proprietary general garden fertilizers of this type are best applied as a preliminary dressing before seed sowing, being worked into the top few inches of soil about seven to ten days previously. Apply the fertilizer evenly, whether it is broadcast or spread in strips where the crop rows will be and, unless sowing instructions state differently, the rate to use is 2 oz. (or a reasonable handful) to the sq. yd. There is more value obtained from applying fertilizer before sowing or planting than at any other time. However, a number of vegetables are all the better for being topdressed with a general fertilizer during the growing season and I like to stick to the policy of giving a little and often. Where dry fertilizers are used they must be sprinkled on the soil carefully, avoiding the leaves of the plants which could be scorched; and if the weather is dry they should be watered in.

Basic slag is also a good fertilizer for use on vegetables since besides being a source of phosphate it contains a certain amount of calcium, which is helpful in breaking down heavy soils. The rate to use is 4 to 6 oz. per sq. yd. and it should be applied during the winter.

LIME Apart from helping to correct soil acidity, applications of chemicals containing lime (or more correctly calcium) will improve the texture of heavy soils by causing the tiny clay particles to clump together. It is advisable that one-third of the vegetable garden should be dressed each year with hydrated lime at the rate of about 3 oz. to the sq. yd. sprinkled over the surface and lightly forked in. On light soils, I would recommend the use of ground limestone for this purpose as this is less easily leached through the soil. On average, this needs to be applied at about twice the rate for hydrated lime.

The best time to apply lime is during the autumn or winter, and at least a month after any manures are added, but in any case not later than mid-February. It should not be used on areas where potatoes are to be grown for it encourages attacks of scab.

Basic Techniques

With one or two exceptions vegetables are grown from seed which is sown either out of doors or under glass. I do think that it is important to buy the best quality seeds as it is pointless to go to a lot of trouble only to experience disappointment when the seeds fail to germinate properly because they are old or otherwise inferior. Store the seeds until sowing time in a cool place and in air-tight tins, so that mice cannot get at them.

Sowing seed out of doors It is an excellent idea to buy your seeds early but, and I do want to stress this, do not be tempted to sow them in the open ground in February or early March even if there is a spell of sunshine and warmish weather then. All too often this is followed by wet, cold conditions and then the seeds rot. If you live in the country, a good guide is to wait until the leaves start showing green in the hedges as this indicates that the soil temperature is rising and seed sowing can begin. As a generalization, I would expect that the sowing times for the first crops will be early March in the South of England, late March in the Midlands and the beginning of April in the North. By placing cloches over the ground where you intend to make early sowings several weeks in advance of the sowing time, the soil will have a chance to warm up a little. It will then be possible to start sowing up to four weeks earlier than the suggested dates. The type of soil also influences the sowing time since lighter soils warm up more quickly than the heavier ones and you should take this into account as well when deciding whether it is safe to start sowing.

Successful germination of the seed and subsequent growth are greatly affected by the state of the seed bed and the type of soil and it is well worthwhile spending time to make sure that both are as good as possible.

The seed bed should be prepared during late winter when the soil is moist but not wet and this is especially important on clay soils where compaction can occur all too easily, adding to the difficulties of obtaining a fine tilth. As I recommended earlier, heavier soils should be dug and left rough for the winter so that the frost and rain can help in breaking down the larger lumps. Any large lumps remaining should be broken down with the back of a fork and the whole plot lightly turned over, large stones and weeds being removed. It is important that the soil should be firm and this can be achieved by treading backwards and forwards over the area. Finally, complete the job by raking the surface to a fine and even finish. Some seeds are tiny and in germination their roots and shoots will have a tough struggle if the seed bed is not up to standard so a firm and level surface is most important. If you are going to use fertilizers always apply them after digging, sprinkling them on so that they mix with the surface soil during firming and raking.

Seeds can be sown broadcast over the seed bed but I much prefer to

Sowing seeds in drills

sow in lines or 'drills' as this makes thinning, weeding and any other jobs which may be necessary so much easier to carry out. A garden line is needed to mark the rows and the drills can be taken out with the corner of a hoe or rake or with a piece of pointed stick.

The depth of the drill depends on the seeds to be sown, and remember when doing this that as a general rule the smaller the seed, the shallower the drill must be. Most vegetable seeds are sown at a depth of $\frac{1}{2}$ in. but peas can be put in $1\frac{1}{2}$ to 2 in. deep, beans 2 in. and beetroot between $\frac{3}{4}$ to 1 in. deep. If the soil is dry, water the drills before sowing.

Sow the seed evenly and thinly in the drills so that there is no unnecessary wastage and the seedlings do not choke each other in the fight for light and air. After sowing fill in the drills by shuffling the soil back with the feet or with the back of a rake and water the rows using a watering can fitted with a rose. The final touch is a label giving details of crop, variety and date sown.

SUCCESSIONAL SOWING One of the easiest mistakes for the beginner to vegetable gardening to make is to have too much of any one crop ready at once so that lettuces run to seed, beans hang unpicked and radishes grow large and uneatable. If you have a deep freezer, this problem can be solved for certain crops – though not lettuce – but otherwise the answer is to sow little and often. Successional sowings can be made of many salad and other vegetable crops at two- or three-week-intervals from March or April onwards to provide enough for the family's requirements at any one time without having a glut and lettuce, spinach, carrots and radishes are examples of vegetables which are best cropped in this way. For example, to maintain a continuous supply of lettuce, you should sow every three weeks from early March or early April (depending on soil temperature) right through until August when a hardy lettuce variety can be sown which will withstand the winter.

THINNING OUT Once the small seedlings appear, they will start competing for light and food and they must usually be thinned to allow adequate space for further development. It is generally best to thin before the seedlings are over 2 in. tall and before the roots have a chance

Thinning out parsnips

to become twined together. For the first thinning, pull out every other plant and when doing this put a finger on the soil either side of the seedling that is to remain as this ensures that its roots are not disturbed when neighbouring plants are pulled up. After about two weeks, or when the rows seem cramped, thin again, and continue to do this until the young plants are spaced as directed in the cultivation instructions for the various crops. Thinnings need not always be discarded, some can be replanted elsewhere and the later ones of such crops as young lettuce, carrots and onions will probably be large enough for eating.

Sowing under glass If a cold frame or unheated greenhouse is available, it is, of course, possible to start sowing sooner than out of doors – in late February or early March. And if you have a greenhouse with some means of heating so that you can keep out the frost, sowing in January is possible. For sowing earlier than January it will be necessary to maintain a temperature of about 13°C. (55°F.) in the greenhouse.

In general, I like to use the John Innes composts for sowing and potting. These are standardized compost mixtures which can be bought ready mixed or prepared at home. There are two basic formulae, one for seeds and one for potting, and the three basic ingredients used in them are soil, peat and sand.

The seed compost is made up of 2 parts by bulk of sterilized soil and 1 part each of peat and coarse sand. To each bushel of this mixture is added 1½ oz. of superphosphate and ¾ oz. of ground limestone.

The potting compost is prepared from 7 parts by bulk of sterilized soil, 3 parts of peat and 2 parts of coarse sand. To this is added a base fertilizer which can be purchased ready mixed or made up from 2 parts by weight of hoof and horn meal, 2 parts of superphosphate and 1 part of sulphate of potash. This is added to the other ingredients at the rate of 4 oz. per bushel for No. 1 compost, 8 oz. per bushel for No. 2 and 12 oz. per bushel for No. 3. To No. 1 add ¾ oz. ground chalk or limestone per bushel, and double and treble this amount for Nos. 2 and 3.

If you are unable to obtain John Innes composts other proprietary seed and potting mixtures can be substituted.

Sow the seed in boxes or pots which have been carefully cleaned or you can use the Jiffystrips of compressed peat pots. An advantage of this method is that there is less disturbance of the roots when planting out. These strips can also be used for pricking out seedlings.

If you are using the conventional wooden seed boxes or clay pots, cover the drainage holes with broken crocks – this is unnecessary with plastic containers – and place a layer of roughage or peat over these before adding the compost. I prefer to use the John Innes seed compost and this should be pressed firm, first with the fingers, particularly along the edges and in the corners, and then with a home-made presser consisting of a flat piece of wood fitted with a handle. This tool is very useful as it gives the compost just the right consistency – not too hard – after the initial firming with the finger tips. The final level of the soil should be such that it reaches to within ¼ to ½ in. of the top of the container. The next stage is to moisten the compost and to do this I fill a container with water and hold the box or pot with its base in the water for just a few minutes. Alternatively, you can water from overhead with a watering can fitted with a fine rose, but I consider the first method more satisfactory.

Sowing seeds in pots

After all this preparation you can begin to sow the seeds by scattering them thinly and evenly over the surface of the compost. Then sieve very fine compost over them to twice the depth of the seeds. After labelling, the containers are ready to be moved to the frame or greenhouse where they must be covered with a pane of glass and a sheet of newspaper until germination takes place. The condensation which forms on the underside of the glass must be wiped away each day. When the seeds have germinated, the newspaper should be removed or the seedlings will become elongated and yellow and when the seedlings touch the glass this should also be removed. Some shade should be given from the sun, however, for the first few days.

As soon as it is possible to handle the seedlings prick them out into boxes filled with John Innes No. 1 potting compost or compressed peat pots, using a dibber to make the holes and taking special care to handle the seedlings by their leaves only and not to damage the fine roots or stems. Aim to plant the seedlings so that their first pair of leaves, known as the seed leaves, are just above the surface of the compost and space them about three inches apart in each direction. The John Innes No. 1 compost has considerably more food value than the mixture in which the seeds were started into growth and, like the seed compost, can be bought ready mixed. As soon as the seedlings are pricked out, water the containers and shade the seedlings from the sun by putting a sheet of newspaper over them for three or four days.

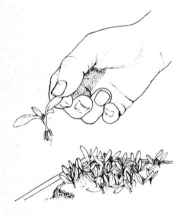

Once the seedlings are established, start the hardening off process by which plants are gradually acclimatized to life in the open air. Put the pots or boxes of young seedlings into a frame and gradually increase the amount of ventilation until after several weeks – the timing depends on the prevailing weather conditions – the lights covering the frames are removed altogether and the young plants can be transplanted into their prepared positions in the garden.

Transplanting Moving plants from the frame to open ground or from one position in the garden to another must be done with care. If possible, choose a cloudy day and water the plants well beforehand. Every effort should be made to avoid too much root disturbance so lift them carefully, retaining a good ball of soil around the roots. This is where the compressed peat pots are particularly useful, as these can be placed directly in the planting holes with no disturbance at all to the plant roots.

Pricking out seedlings

Using a trowel or dibber make the planting holes, which should be large enough to contain the roots comfortably. If the soil is dry fill the holes with water and allow it to soak in. This will provide enough moisture in the adjacent soil to hold the plants for a few days. Set the plants so that the new soil line is slightly higher on the stem than the previous mark and replace the soil around the roots, making it firm enough to give the plants a good footing but not so firm that the roots are restricted.

Some plants transplant easily, examples include all the brassica crops, lettuces, tomatoes, celery, beans and peas but turnips, carrots and beetroot, in fact all root crops, should be sown directly in the ground where they are to grow and thinned.

Transplanting can also be used as a way of obtaining a succession of cropping. When sowing lettuce, I sow the seed only one quarter of the way across the intended row and then transplant the thinnings from this portion to the next quarter row. A few weeks later I sow the third quarter and once again use the thinnings to plant the last quarter. In each case the transplanted lettuce are usually 10 to 14 days later in maturing than those left undisturbed, so in this way a succession of cropping is created.

Aftercare of seedlings and young plants Once the seedlings have emerged, or the young plants have been transplanted to their cropping positions, then prompt and frequent attention to hoeing and watering is important. In the first few weeks it is particularly critical to remove all weeds as soon as they appear and before they can compete with the vegetable seedlings or young plants. This can be done either by hand pulling or by using an implement such as the Dutch hoe, but do remember to keep all cultivation shallow as the vegetable roots are likely to be near the soil surface.

I think that the hoe should be used more in the vegetable plot than in any other part of the garden. It is a most valuable tool not only for keeping down weeds but also for stirring the soil. This in turn stimulates growth by letting air into the soil and the loose surface layer so formed acts as a dust mulch preventing loss of moisture from the lower layers of soil.

There are several different types of hoe but I consider the following four are the most important. The Dutch hoe has a narrow flat blade almost in line with the handle and is especially useful for weeding as the operator walks backwards when using it and so does not tread over the freshly hoed soil. The draw hoe has a blade set at right angles to the handle, and it is used to make drills for seed sowing, to destroy tough weeds by using it with a chopping action and for earthing up potatoes. This tool is available in a swan-necked version or with a straight connection to the handle. A hand hoe is a tool of the draw hoe type with the typical swan neck but with a short handle and is excellent for close work among plants such as thinning seedlings and weeding. Finally, the Canterbury hoe which has prongs instead of a blade and these are also set at right angles to the handle. This is a good tool for breaking down clods and for loosening the surface of hard soil. If you have to make a choice between these hoes, then the Dutch hoe would be the most generally useful.

Most vegetables are thirsty plants and a shortage of water leads to poor development and unsatisfactory yields. As I have already said, good soil cultivation with the incorporation of organic matter will help

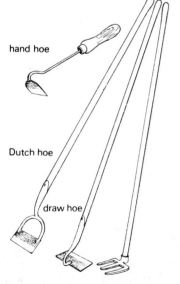

hand hoe

Dutch hoe

draw hoe

Canterbury hoe

Types of hoe

considerably towards maintaining a moisture-retaining soil, but generous watering is very important. However, this may be easier said than done because during prolonged periods of dry weather there may be a shortage of mains water, but if you can get it then I think the most essential plants to water (and in order of priority) are – runner beans, celery, newly planted out brassica crops, peas and onions, if you want large specimens.

When applying water, and this can be done with either a hose or watering can, it is important that the soil is thoroughly soaked. This will help water retention at a lower level and encourage the roots to burrow downwards. Spasmodic shallow watering tempts the roots to spread out close to the surface where they will be easily damaged by the hoe and will have little resistance to drought. On average, I like to water thoroughly once a week and I would emphasize here that the water should be applied in a fairly gentle slow spray so that it has a chance to seep properly into the soil. If it is given with too much force, it will run off the surface and possibly carry some of the topsoil with it.

Storing and Freezing
One of the big advantages of growing your own vegetables is that it is possible to enjoy the fruits of your labours throughout the winter months because, if kept under proper conditions, vegetables will retain their flavour long after harvesting. This does not apply to all crops but most of the root crops will store very successfully and many other vegetables can be frozen.

Indoor and outdoor storing An airy frostproof shed or dry cellar is an ideal location for storing such crops as potatoes, carrots, beetroots, celeriac, salsify, scorzonera, swede, turnips, parsnips and kohl-rabi. Where applicable, the tops should be cut off and the roots stored either in boxes or in heaps and covered with fine soil, sand or peat. Many of these vegetables are winter hardy and can also be stored in a sheltered place in the garden where they should again be covered with soil or sand.

Onions, shallots, pumpkins and marrows can also be kept in a frostproof shed but these should be hung in bunches or nets or placed on slatted shelves so that the air can circulate freely around them. In the

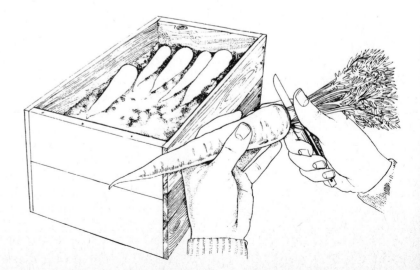

Storing carrots in boxes

case of onions and shallots make sure the bulbs have been dried off properly and with all the roots be careful to store only sound, undamaged specimens. I think it is advisable to examine stored vegetables at intervals to make sure that no fungal diseases are developing which might spread and ruin all.

Deep freezing This is an excellent way of storing excess crops for later use, particularly those which can only be produced over a short season. In my opinion, the best of all the vegetables for deep freezing are peas, broad beans, runner beans, brussels sprouts and cauliflowers, in that order. I do not think that there is any point in deep freezing those crops which you can have from the garden or from store throughout the year.

For freezing, all vegetables should be harvested when they are young and tender and should then be prepared immediately. Certain varieties are particularly suitable – we find that the peas Little Marvel and Onward freeze exceptionally well – and now some of the seed firms are producing varieties which are especially good for freezing and these are indicated in the catalogues.

Exhibiting

The growing of vegetables for exhibition is a very specialized procedure and rather outside the scope of this book. It requires a lot of hard work and extra care in the preparation of the soil, in the sowing of seeds and special methods of culture for many of the crops.

However, if you would like to enter some of the classes at local vegetable shows, the following points may provide an indication of the sort of thing the judge will be looking for. First, read the show schedule carefully and make sure that if a class states 'ten runner beans' you do enter ten and not nine or eleven. This may sound elementary but very often people are disqualified for their failure to follow such instructions precisely.

Take care in lifting and cleaning root crops; for example, use soft cloths not scrubbing brushes to clean carrots and potatoes so that the skins are not scratched. Do not peel onions too much and do not polish tomatoes or cucumbers as this disturbs the natural bloom on the fruit. In the same way, pick and handle peas by the stalks only or you will mark the pods. Runner beans, broad beans and peas should be picked when they are young. Beetroots are judged on colour as well as size and quality, carrots on size, colour and quality, potatoes on cleanliness and evenness of size and onions and shallots on evenness of size and quality.

Pests and Diseases

There are a large number of pests and diseases which attack vegetables but I shall give here only the ones most likely to be seen and to cause trouble. All garden chemicals must be applied at the correct strengths and at the right time and I cannot emphasize too strongly the need to read carefully the manufacturers' instructions on all chemicals. I do not like spraying any more than I have to but a certain amount has to be done to keep vegetables free from pests and diseases. Many of the diseases, in fact, can be kept at bay by employing good methods of cultivation and ensuring that the plants grow strongly. Try also to be ahead of the enemy by watching for early signs of attack and taking preventive measures before the pest or disease has a chance to gain a foothold.

It is especially important when dealing with food crops to observe the correct periods of time which must be allowed to elapse between application and harvesting and, even more important, to be fully aware of the prohibition of certain chemicals on specific crops. For example, BHC has a tainting effect and should not be used as a soil insecticide where any of the root crops are grown. Gamma BHC (lindane) has a far less tainting effect but still must not be used on potatoes.

Observe also the need to protect children and animals from the effects of the chemicals by storing these well out of reach and, again, taking care in their application. Bees can be killed by pesticides as easily as the insects which they are intended to control so try to do the spraying in the evening after the bees have finished their day's work.

There is now a range of garden sprayers available which should suit all needs and pockets but care must be taken to wash well all equipment used for chemicals and not to use it for other purposes.

With regard to the chemicals themselves, the manufacturers have prepared a number of multi-purpose sprays and dusts which make mixing and other preparation relatively foolproof provided, of course, the instructions are read carefully. In the list of pests and diseases which follows I have suggested various remedies, many of these will be found under various trade names and there are other chemicals available.

Pests

Aphids A general name covering a range of insects which includes the greenfly and blackfly. These tiny lice-like insects (in fact, often called plant lice) are barely $\frac{1}{16}$ in. long and occur in both winged and wingless forms. Generally they centre their attacks on young shoots and the undersides of young leaves and they seriously weaken plants by sucking the sap, causing leaves to become distorted and fall prematurely. This has the effect of checking growth.

CONTROL Spray with malathion, BHC, menazon, derris or pyrethrum when an attack is noticed and make sure that the chemical comes directly into contact with the insects.

Blackfly is a particular problem on broad beans and, in this case, apart from spraying with menazon, derris or pyrethrum, a degree of control can be gained by early sowing and by pinching out the growing tips when the flowers have been set.

Cabbage caterpillars These are the larvae of the familiar cabbage white butterfly and the lesser-known cabbage moth, which flies by night. They feed voraciously, attacking the leaves of cabbages and other brassicas in summer and can completely skeletonize the plants in a few days if no attempt is made to check them.

The cabbage white butterfly is creamy white; it lays its eggs on the undersurfaces of the leaves and the caterpillars which hatch out are green. The cabbage moth is grey and brown with darker markings and its caterpillars are green or reddish-brown, an interesting distinguishing feature is that they coil themselves up when disturbed.

CONTROL The best way to control the caterpillars is by hand picking whenever possible. Alternatively, you can spray or dust the plants with derris or carbaryl.

Cabbage root fly The larvae of this fly are small white grubs which attack the lower part of the stem or upper roots of brassica crops and cause the leaves to assume a leaden colour; the plants eventually wilt and collapse. The fly appears from May onwards and the eggs are laid on the stems just below the surface of the soil. Newly planted seedlings are especially vulnerable to attack.

CONTROL The seed bed should be dusted with gamma BHC and newly planted seedlings with 4 per cent. calomel dust, repeating this application a fortnight later. Alternatively, the roots of the young plants can be dipped in a paste, made from calomel dust and water, before planting. This will also act as a control for club root.

Carrot fly The greenish-black flies lay their eggs in the soil during spring and summer and small white maggots hatch out. It is these grubs which attack the roots and do all the damage, and this can be very extensive even to the point of making the roots worthless. This pest is most troublesome in late April and throughout May, and carrots sown in June and July often escape damage because few flies are about then.

CONTROL Dust naphthalene on the surface soil around plants every 10 days, from thinning time until the end of June, or in the early seedling stages dust with gamma BHC.

Celery fly This small fly lays its eggs on the undersides of the celery leaves during spring and summer and immediately on hatching the tiny white or green grubs work their way into the leaf tissues. Once there they feed, leaving the characteristic whitish blisters or trails which give rise to the alternative name for this pest of celery leaf miner. In a bad attack the tunnelling in the leaves may be so severe that only the skin remains.

CONTROL Mild attacks can be controlled by picking off and burning affected leaves, but usually it is necessary to spray occasionally from May to August with malathion or BHC.

Eelworms These are microscopic transparent eel-like creatures which attack some plants by entering the tissues and feeding and multiplying there. A range of decorative plants as well as fruit and vegetable crops are affected. Roots, bulbs and tubers can be infected by eelworms entering from the soil, while the leaves are infected by eelworms entering through the breathing pores.

Potatoes are attacked by an eelworm which produces tiny white cysts on the roots and tubers, causing the leaves to turn yellow and ultimately checking growth. The cysts are a means of re-infecting clean soil. In the case of onions, the eelworms pass to the stems from the bulbs and bring about swelling and misshapen growth.

CONTROL As they can be seen only with the aid of a microscope or strong hand lens, they are difficult to control but fortunately most individual species of eelworm confine their attention to particular crops, and this does assist control. Crop rotation comes in here, and where the soil is found to be contaminated, the crop concerned should not be grown in the same piece of ground for several years. Destroy all infected plants and keep down weeds which may act as hosts – chickweed, for example, acts as host for the onion eelworm.

Flea beetle This small blackish beetle, about ⅛ in. long, is capable of jumping a long way when disturbed. Flea beetles attack the seedlings and young plants of cabbage and other brassicas, turnip, and radish, eating small circular holes in the leaves and entirely destroying them if not checked. The beetle is most troublesome on light sandy soils in dry weather when it can do a tremendous amount of damage, particularly to seedlings. It is not nearly such a problem in dull or damp weather.

CONTROL One method of preventing an attack is to encourage seedlings to make really good vigorous growth by watering, hoeing and the use of artificial fertilizers. Dust the seedlings occasionally with gamma BHC, derris or malathion.

Mice These hardly need any description and they often do a lot of damage to early sown peas and beans, and root crops in store.

CONTROL The best way is to use one of the proprietary mouse poisons but it must be kept away from children, animals and birds and I find the best way to do this is to place the poison in the middle of a small piece of drain pipe (one of the land-drain type) and put this between the rows of crops. In store use poison or traps.

Pigeons These birds are a menace as far as all the brassica crops and seedling peas are concerned. I have tried all the favourite ways of deterring them such as hanging up bottles and tinfoil but I find the only effective method is by well-supported netting placed over the crops. It is usually in autumn and winter that pigeons do the worst damage so if you have fruit nets these can be switched to the vegetable garden in the autumn. Nylon netting will not deteriorate with the weather.

Onion fly This is a major pest of onions and it resembles the ordinary house fly in appearance, laying its eggs in spring and summer near the bottom of young onion plants. The white maggots attack the young bulbs, eating into them and destroying the roots. The first indication of such an attack is that the foliage turns yellow and flags. The bulbs usually contain maggots, sometimes in large numbers, and are unusable.

CONTROL This pest is not easy to control but dusting the soil with calomel, BHC or lindane immediately after planting and again two weeks later will help to discourage an attack. Remove and burn damaged plants and treat the seed before sowing with calomel.

Red spider mites Although these minute reddish creatures can only just be seen with the naked eye they can do a great deal of damage by sucking the sap of plants. The leaves become mottled, lose their colour and fall prematurely. Red spider mites are especially likely to be a problem in hot dry weather, and under glass much can be done to prevent attack by maintaining a damp atmosphere.
CONTROL Spray with derris, malathion or dimethoate and fumigate glasshouses with azobenzene and diazinon or use malathion aerosols.

Slugs The worst of the slugs is the little keeled slug which lives in the soil, and the crops which suffer most are celery and potatoes.
CONTROL All are difficult to control. The main methods are: by using a soil fumigant such as naphthalene; by putting down bait; or by using one of the slug repellants that are watered in. The bait should never be scattered over the garden where it can be picked up easily by birds and domestic animals. Instead put it down in small piles and place a tile or slate over each pile. If the tile is slightly tilted, the slugs will be able to get underneath but animals and birds will not.

Whitefly These tiny winged insects can be especially troublesome on cucumbers and tomatoes under glass, while a related species attacks members of the cabbage family. The adult fly lays eggs on the leaves and these develop into scale-like creatures which suck the sap and weaken the plants. In addition, the leaves become coated with sticky grey excrement which stops them breathing.
CONTROL Under glass, fumigate with tetrachlorethane, use a malathion aerosol or spray with malathion. Outdoors, spray with gamma BHC or malathion.

Wireworm The larva of a type of beetle known as a 'click' beetle because of the clicking noise it makes with its wings. The adult beetles are brown and the thin worm-like grubs are about 1 in. long with hard, shiny, yellow skins. They are found in large numbers in grassland, and where this is dug up and planted with vegetables, they will attack and feed on potatoes, carrots and other root crops doing considerable damage by destroying the smaller roots and boring tunnels in the larger ones. This may be severe in spring and early autumn.
CONTROL They can be trapped by burying pieces of potatoes or carrots attached to wooden skewers, so that they can be easily located, close to the crops and examining these frequently; deterred by forking in naphthalene or killed by dusting the soil with BHC where there is no danger of tainting of crops such as carrot or potato. Seed should be treated with an organo-mercury seed dressing before sowing.

Diseases
Botrytis The common name for this disease – grey mould – comes from the grey spores of the fungus which form a mould on the leaves and stems of the plants. The attacked tissues then decay.
CONTROL To keep down the spread of the disease, improve air circulation and try to prevent the atmosphere getting too humid. Careful watering and an increase in heat will help to control it under glass. Out

of doors, crops should be gathered before the weather becomes wet and cold and stored in dry, airy places. Spray with thiram or a systemic fungicide.

Broad bean chocolate spot This is a form of botrytis which is seen as large dark brown blotches on the leaves, and streaks on the stems. It is more severe after very cold or wet weather and so is more common on autumn-sown beans.
CONTROL Where the disease appears spray the plants with Bordeaux mixture.

Celery leaf spot The fungus which causes this disease is carried on seed but all reputable seedsmen sell seed which has been treated against it. The disease spreads rapidly in damp weather and can be very destructive. It shows up as brown spots on the leaves, which wither and die.
CONTROL Spray with Bordeaux mixture or zineb if the disease is seen and repeat at fortnightly intervals until October.

Club root Also known as finger and toe and anbury, this fungal disease is probably the best known of all vegetable diseases. It affects cabbages and other brassicas, making the roots swollen, distorted and almost fibreless. Eventually the roots decay and an evil smell can be detected. Infected plants must be burnt and the soil should not be planted with brassicas or other plants susceptible to the disease for at least four years. Farmyard manure can also be a means of bringing the disease into the garden if the animals which provide the litter have been fed on swedes or any member of the brassica family which has been affected with club root. Club root is caused by one of the slime fungi and these are very difficult to eradicate.
CONTROL Soil that is acid or 'sour' is highly favourable for the development of the disease and should be heavily limed at the rate of 6 to 8 oz. per sq. yd., as soon as the infected plants have been cleared. Similar dressings should be given annually for three or four years. As an additional precaution, dip the roots of the seedlings before planting into a paste made of 4 per cent. calomel dust and water, or sprinkle calomel dust along the drills or into the planting holes.

Damping off This fungal disease, which occurs under glass, attacks seedlings just above soil level, with the result that they collapse. The trouble can often occur over large patches in the seed boxes. It is most likely to be troublesome where seeds are sown too thickly and it spreads quickly in stuffy damp conditions.
CONTROL The best method is to sow thinly and prick off as soon as possible. Watering seedlings with a solution of Cheshunt compound will prevent spread.

Mildew This is a fungal disease which attacks numerous crops. The surfaces of the leaves, and possibly also the stems, become covered with whitish or greyish patches that often appear to be mealy. Mildew is most likely to occur when the atmosphere is moist and the soil is rather dry, and it is common in August and September. The plants are not usually killed outright but growth is weakened.
CONTROL This includes dusting the leaves with flowers of sulphur or spraying with colloidal sulphur, Bordeaux mixture or zineb. Brassicas, spinach, peas, lettuce and onions are particularly likely to be attacked.

Neck rot One of the botrytis group of fungi which causes the neck or top of the onion bulb to turn brown and become soft. Later the decayed part develops grey mould. This disease is particularly prevalent among stored bulbs.

CONTROL The bulbs should be properly ripened before lifting and dried well. Store in dry, cool conditions and spread them well out. Onions with thick, soft necks are the most likely to be affected.

Parsnip canker This is recognized as brown, or sometimes black, patches which can be seen around the top of parsnip roots. There are various contributory causes; the roots may crack from the action of rain after dry weather and this leads to infection which brings about rotting. Injury by carrot fly larvae also encourages rotting.

CONTROL Where the trouble has occurred previously, give the soil a generous application of lime before sowing seed. Do not grow parsnips on heavily manured ground. Canker is sometimes started off by injuries originally caused by the carrot fly larvae and in this respect an application of 4 per cent. calomel dust is useful.

Potato blight This disease of potatoes and tomatoes is unfortunately all too prevalent, but it is unlikely to cause trouble on early potatoes as it does not usually affect plants until early July in most parts of Britain. It does little damage in dry seasons but can quickly cause devastation of the crop in a mild wet season.

The disease is easily identified as moist brown or black patches on the leaves. These spread rapidly to the stems which eventually die. Potato tubers turn brown and rot; tomato fruits become marked with decaying brown patches and also rot.

CONTROL A preventive spray of Bordeaux mixture or zineb should be applied in early July just before an attack is likely and this should be repeated at fortnightly intervals until the middle of September. Some varieties are more susceptible than others.

Potato scab This trouble is identified by the brown, flaky scabs on the skin of the tuber. The quality of the tubers for cooking is not affected, but it does make them more difficult to clean and peel satisfactorily. Be sure to burn the peelings of damaged tubers instead of returning them to the compost heap. It is likely to occur in light soils lacking in organic matter or in soils containing a lot of lime, and surrounding the planting sets with peat or garden compost will help to overcome this trouble.

Potato wart disease This is the most serious disease of potatoes and is easily recognized by wart-like outgrowths on the tubers and stem bases. The flesh is attacked also and the potatoes may be destroyed completely. There is no known cure but many varieties are immune to it, and where the disease is at all prevalent, these varieties should be grown exclusively. As this is a notifiable disease in Britain, if your plants do become infected you must report it to the Ministry of Agriculture, Fisheries and Food.

Root-rot A fungus disease affecting tomatoes grown under glass which results in the plants flagging. The wilting starts at the top of the plant, unlike verticillium wilt (page 33) with which it might otherwise be confused. Root-rot is encouraged by over-watering, poor drainage and low soil temperature.

CONTROL A topdressing of peat will encourage fresh root production and if this is combined with overhead damping of the plants and shading of the house, a measure of control will be obtained.

Soft rot A bacterial disease which attacks many vegetables and is sometimes caused by deficiencies of such trace elements as boron and magnesium. The tissues in the centre of the plant or root turn brown and decay rapidly, becoming very wet and slimy and sometimes foul smelling. The victims eventually disintegrate into a liquid mess. The bacterium responsible is thought to be transmitted by slugs, celery fly or through damage to the plants.

Once infected there is no cure, but growing the plants strongly, keeping the ground clean, avoiding injury to roots or top growth and controlling slugs and other pests will do a lot to prevent this trouble occurring. The rot also affects stored roots, so take care to store only sound ones.

Stem rot This disease, which affects tomatoes, cucumbers and melons, causes the stem to rot just above soil level. The flow of sap is checked and the plant wilts suddenly and collapses. Concentric black rings develop on the lower fruits of older tomato plants. The disease is often caused by over-deep planting and by water collecting at the base of the stems. A way of overcoming over-moist conditions at the base of the stem is to plant on low mounds and maintain higher temperatures.
CONTROL When trouble occurs, dust heavily around the stems with copper fungicide, thiram or captan. Mulching soil with peat or straw helps to prevent fungus spores splashing up on to fruits.

Tomato blossom end rot A physiological disorder which is seen first as a dark flattish, sometimes shrunken area on the end furthest from the stalk of the fruit, although it is present on the inside of the fruit before this. This rot occurs mainly on the first-formed fruits and is caused by insufficient water reaching them. Vigorous plants with large soft leaves are the most liable to be attacked as on such plants the leaves tend to absorb moisture which should be going to the fruits. This type of plant is produced by too much nitrogen in the soil so careful attention to balanced feeding is important.
CONTROL The best method of preventing the trouble is to give regular supplies of water and to aim at maintaining well-balanced growth with a good root system which can take up sufficient water for both leaves and fruit.

Tomato blotchy ripening This is the term given to a condition of tomatoes in which the fruit becomes blotched with hard green or yellow patches instead of ripening to an even red. It may be due to potash deficiency and then may often be corrected by two or three applications of sulphate of potash, applied at up to 2 oz. per sq. yd. The best way of preventing it, however, is to make use of balanced fertilizer treatment before planting and to aim at establishing a good root system and maintaining adequate soil moisture so that the plant can take up the necessary potash. Blotchy ripening may also occur when fruits are unduly exposed to the rays of the sun through the glass.

Tomato leaf mould This is a fungal disease which causes a lot of trouble on tomatoes grown under glass. Pale yellow spots appear on the upper surface. The disease spreads rapidly in hot, moist conditions and the leaves may wither completely.

CONTROL Ventilation and good air circulation are important counter-measures and affected leaves should be removed. Spraying with zineb will also help.

Verticillium wilt An alternative name for this is sleepy disease. It affects tomatoes resulting in severe wilting and yellowing of the plants. It is usually caused by the fungus *Verticillium albo-atrum* which attacks the roots and base of the plant eventually infecting the sap and the plant dies. Although its effects are very much the same as those produced by root-rot it can be identified by the fact that in sleepy disease the wilting normally occurs in the lower leaves first, whereas with root-rot the wilting usually begins at the top of the plant. Another difference is that, unlike root-rot, this trouble is most obvious in cool air and soil conditions. Internal discolouration of the stem, which with root-rot only affects the lower few inches, may reach to the top of the plant.
CONTROL Keep the greenhouse shaded and as warm as possible and damp the plants frequently overhead rather than watering too much at the roots. If the house can be maintained at a temperature of at least 25°C. (77°F.) for a fortnight, a complete cure may sometimes be affected. Dead plants must be removed immediately and if new ones are to take their place, the soil should be watered with Cheshunt compound before planting.

Virus There are many kinds of viruses which affect a wide range of plants and produce so many different symptoms that they are among the most difficult of plant diseases to identify. Any plant which is stunted or develops dry brown spots and streaks on stems and leaves should be treated with suspicion. Other symptoms show up as yellow mottled leaves or leaves which are deformed or twisted.
CONTROL As there is no cure for viruses the best course of action is to destroy and burn all infected plants. Another important point is to keep the plants free from aphids and other sucking insects, because they can transfer viruses from one plant to another.

Vegetables and How to Grow Them

In the following list of vegetables I have given you practical growing instructions for all the popular crops and have also included a few of the 'novelty' crops which are gaining in popularity in Britain. In this group I am thinking mainly of aubergine, peppers, pumpkins and sweet corn. Other vegetables which are not widely grown and deserve to have much more attention paid to them are the good winter salad crops such as endive and chicory, and the unusual scorzonera, salsify and seakale.

I have endeavoured to give some indication of the yield which can be expected from as many of the crops as possible. This is always difficult as local factors as well as the choice of variety must be taken into account when assessing the final result. I advise, therefore, that you consider the figures given to be the average yield and to remember that with good soil and favourable weather it will very often be possible to exceed this.

Flavour as well as crop yields will be affected by different soils and it is well worth finding out which vegetables do best in your district. So, join a local horticultural society or talk to local gardeners and make use of their experience, as well as doing some experimenting yourself. When choosing varieties it is worth remembering that those which are favoured by commercial growers because they give high yields with a minimum of trouble, are not necessarily the kinds with the best flavour and this, after all, should be the main consideration when you are growing vegetables for your own table.

A final point with regard to the information given in the following list of vegetables, where a crop is particularly liable to attack from pests and disease this is mentioned under the heading 'What goes wrong' and in the majority of cases descriptions of symptoms and control measure will be found on pages 26 to 33.

Artichoke, Globe

SOW March under glass
April outdoors
PLANT Offsets in early April
HARVEST From the second year after planting in late summer

This vegetable is a very decorative plant (in fact, a relative of the thistle) which is grown for its large edible flower heads.

Position Fairly rich and heavy well-dug soil in an open, sunny place.
Cultivation Plants can be raised from seed sown under glass in March or out of doors in April. However, a more satisfactory method is to plant offsets which are obtainable from the nurseryman or can be detached from established plants – preferably those known to be good croppers. These offsets should be planted in April and spaced 3 ft. apart in each direction.

Artichokes are heavy feeders so spread manure or compost around the plants in May and remember to remove any flower stems which are formed during the first summer. This will encourage the formation of a large plant by the following year. In the autumn any dead leaves can be cut away and the crowns protected with bracken or straw.

Well-grown runner beans

35

Once danger of frost is passed in spring, remove the protection and feed the plants with a high nitrogen fertilizer. Two or three additional doses of fertilizer should be given during the season.

The plants produce their best crops in their second and third years. Pick the flower heads regularly as soon as they are plump and before they open. Cut approximately $1\frac{1}{2}$ in. below the head.

Varieties Green Globe.

What goes wrong Artichokes suffer attacks from several types of aphid – both greenfly and blackfly. It is not really safe to spray plants once the buds are formed so flower heads must be well washed before cooking.

Slugs and snails can also be a nuisance and if given the opportunity may eat the buds before you have a chance to.

Artichoke, Jerusalem

PLANT In February
HARVEST The following autumn and winter
STORE In a cool, airy shed or leave in the ground and dig as required

These are grown for their knobbly tuberous roots which are cooked and served in a similar manner to potatoes. The plants grow to 6 ft. and make a good summer windbreak or temporary screen to conceal compost heaps or other less attractive garden features. The flowers look like perennial sunflowers.

Position Jerusalem artichokes are hardy and easy plants which will grow in ordinary soil and either an open position or partial shade but better roots will be produced if the soil has been dressed with compost or manure.

Cultivation The tubers are planted in February, 3 in. deep and 15 in. apart. Allow 3 ft. between rows. Jerusalem artichokes are good-tempered vegetables and demand little attention but hoe them occasionally, drawing the soil towards the rows to make slight ridges. In late October cut the top growth down to ground level.

Lift the tubers as required in autumn and winter, or lift and store in autumn as for potatoes. It is advisable to set aside some of the tubers for replanting the following year.

What goes wrong Very little, slugs sometimes feed on the tubers.

Asparagus

PLANT April
HARVEST Spring and early summer, third year after planting onwards
YIELD 5 lb. to a 10-ft. row

Asparagus is a hardy vegetable with a delicious flavour, which, when once established, will crop for many years.

Position This is a crop which needs a deeply dug soil, well manured with rotted compost or manure and with a liberal dressing of bonemeal. Very good drainage is an essential. I prefer to plant in single rows and to earth up the plants later, like potatoes.

Cultivation The young plants (often known as crowns) should be set out in April 3 to 4 in. deep, 15 in. apart in rows 2 ft. apart and I find it is best to buy one-year-old crowns. Asparagus should be regarded as a long-term vegetable and consequently it needs a little extra effort. During the first year do not cut any spears but allow all the shoots to grow and produce foliage as this will build up the size of the plants. Keep the beds weed free and feed with a little general fertilizer during the summer. Good supplies of water must be given in dry weather. Cut down all top growth in the first week of November and apply a dressing of well-rotted manure or compost. Before growth starts the following spring draw some soil up alongside the plants – rather as if you are earthing up potatoes. In late February I like to feed my plants with agricultural salt at the rate of 2 oz. to the sq. yd. During the second season, continue cultural operations as for the first year.

Cutting asparagus spears

Cutting can begin in the third year. Use a sharp serrated knife, or a special asparagus knife, and cut the spears when they are about 4 in. above soil level. The cuts should be made well below soil level at approximately 2 in. from the crowns. Do not continue the cutting season after June 15th; allow the foliage to grow as this will manufacture food for the roots and so ensure that the following year's crop will be good. The ferny growths should be cut down in early November when the bed is given a dressing of well-rotted manure.

Asparagus can also be increased by sowing seeds in light soil in rows 1 in. deep in early April. Thin the seedlings to 12 in. apart and transplant them to their permanent positions the following April. It will be another two or three seasons before any spears will be ready for harvesting.

Varieties These include Martha Washington, Connover's Colossal, Market Favourite and Suttons' Perfection.

What goes wrong Earwigs and slugs can be a problem. Also the asparagus beetle, the larvae of which feed on the foliage and in a bad attack will leave the stems bare. The adult beetle is small, black with orange markings and the larvae are grey-green grubs. Control by spraying with derris or malathion.

Aubergine (Egg Plant)

SOW January and February
HARVEST August
YIELD 4 to 6 fruits to each plant

This unusual vegetable, also known as egg plant, is a relative of the peppers and tomatoes. The large oval fruits are very beautiful with shiny purplish-black skins and a superb flavour when cooked.

Position Aubergines are half-hardy plants and must be raised under glass though in warmer areas they can be transplanted out of doors once the danger of frosts is passed provided the site chosen is warm and sunny and protected. They require a loose, fertile and well-drained soil.

Cultivation Sow the seeds in January or February in a warm greenhouse, temperature 16°C. (60°F.). After germination the seedlings should be pricked out and then potted singly into 3-in. pots. At this stage the young plants can either be hardened off for planting outside or, if you have sufficient room in a greenhouse or in frames, then gradually pot the plants on until they reach the 6- or 7-in. size pot in John Innes No. 3 compost. Pinch out the growing tips when the plants are about 6 in. high but do not at the moment remove any of the side shoots. Once the fruits have set restrict each plant to between four and six fruits, then remove excess flowers and stop all the side shoots. Aubergines should be kept growing steadily so water freely and feed with a liquid fertilizer once or twice during the growing season.

The fruits should be ready for harvesting from August. It is important to handle them carefully, as they bruise easily, and to pick them before the skin loses its shine. After this, the fruits will be tough and the seeds become bitter.

For outdoor cultivation, harden off the plants and plant outside in late May, spacing them 2 ft. apart in each direction. Then cultural treatment is identical to that of greenhouse-grown plants except that you will have to give some attention to the need for frequent hoeing.

Varieties Long purple.

What goes wrong The only pest which is likely to give trouble is the red spider mite and as this thrives in a hot dry atmosphere it is unlikely to be a problem on the outdoor crops. In the greenhouse maintain a moist atmosphere and fumigate with azobenzene or spray with malathion.

Beans, Broad

SOW Main crops from February to July

Early crops in November in warm, sheltered positions

HARVEST June to October

YIELD 5 lb. to a 10-ft. row

STORE By freezing

Broad beans are an easily grown vegetable cultivated for the large edible seeds within the pods. They are classified in three groups: long-pods (hardier and better for early sowing in autumn and spring), Windsors (better flavour) and the dwarf varieties.

Position Rich, well-manured soil which has been dressed with general fertilizer about a week before sowing.

Cultivation Sow the seeds 4 to 6 in. apart in drills 2 in. deep and allow 3 ft. between rows. Longpod varieties such as Aquadulce, and also the dwarf variety The Sutton, are suitable for sowing in November in areas where the winter is not too severe. But it is wise to wait until late March before starting to sow Windsor varieties out of doors. The Sutton is a good variety for late sowing and I find it makes a useful catch crop for sowing in July after early potatoes or winter greens. It will produce beans for picking from late August into October.

If you have a greenhouse or frames then you can sow broad beans, as I do, in late February and early March – one seed to a pot or spaced 2 to 3 in. apart in a box and using John Innes No. 1 compost. These can be planted outside in April and if the weather is cold then I put cloches over them.

Pinch out the growing tips when the beans have set their flowers as this discourages blackfly – always a problem with this crop. Water late crops well in dry weather and support the taller varieties on string strained between posts which are placed at each end of the row. Alternatively, use pea sticks or the plastic netting which is sold specially for this purpose.

The pods grow to a length of between 6 and 12 in. and should be picked as soon as they reach a usable size. Pick often to keep the beans coming.

When cropping is finished, cut the tops down and, if possible, leave the roots in the soil as they are a valuable source of nitrogen. This also applies to all the pea and bean crops but if you are following them immediately with another crop then dig the roots out and put them on the compost heap.

Varieties Aquadulce, a longpod variety, is one of the most useful for autumn and early spring sowing. The Windsor varieties are the best for bottling and freezing. The Sutton is a good dwarf variety, suitable for autumn, spring and summer growing.

What goes wrong Blackfly (aphid) is the most common problem, they are found in massed clumps along the stems and leaves. Chocolate spot is the most likely disease.

Removing tip of plant as a control against blackfly

Beans, French

SOW January or February under glass

Late April and May to June outside

HARVEST July to October (main crop)

YIELD 2 lb. to a 10-ft. row

STORE By freezing

Carrot, Nantes variety

There are two types of french bean – the dwarf and the climbing. The former requires no staking and is, therefore, especially useful to the gardener.

Position The ground should be well dug and rotted manure or garden compost incorporated. A dressing of a general fertilizer should be given a week or so before sowing.

Cultivation As soon as you think your soil is warm enough in May, sow the seeds thinly 1 in. deep and allow at least 2 ft. between the rows. Thin the resulting seedlings to 6 in. apart. The climbing varieties should be grown in rows 3 ft. apart and provided with pea sticks or netting for support. The important thing to remember is that french beans do not like a cold seed bed and the sowing date can be hastened by covering the soil with cloches for a couple of weeks before sowing. Alternatively, seeds can be sown under cloches in April. A late sowing in June will produce a crop in late September and early October, and the cropping period can be extended even further by a July sowing in frames or in a position which can be covered with cloches so that the plants can be given protection in the late autumn.

Hoe regularly and water well in dry weather. When the flowers appear spray the plants regularly with water to help them to set.

Pick frequently as soon as the beans are a usable size (3 to 4 in.) and do not allow any to mature and produce seed as this checks further cropping.

To obtain early crops, sow the seeds under glass in January or February. I usually put five in a 3-in. pot of John Innes No. 1 compost and germinate them at a temperature of 13°C. (55°F.). Repot them into 7-in. pots of John Innes No. 3 compost. It is amazing the number of beans which can be picked from 10 or 12 pots. Alternatively, harden the young plants off for planting out in early June.

Varieties Scarlet Prince and Canadian Wonder are good for sowing in pots. Other useful varieties include The Prince and Masterpiece and I recommend Sprite, which is a stringless variety. Of the climbing sorts I like Purple Podded.

What goes wrong As a general rule, french beans are not subject to too much trouble but watch out for blackfly and red spider mite.

Beans, Runner

SOW April to May
HARVEST July to October
YIELD 40 lb. to a 10-ft. row
STORE By freezing or salting

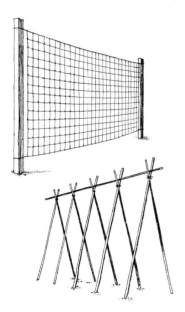

Supports for runner beans

Runner beans are one of my favourites and the most attractive of the vegetables when growing. They can be used with advantage to screen compost heaps or unsightly buildings and they are easily grown to maturity in large pots, tubs or other suitably deep containers. There are both red- and white-flowered varieties.

Position A fairly rich soil – obtained by digging an 18-in. wide, 12-in. deep trench in February or March and working well-rotted manure or garden compost into the bottom. The soil is then returned together with a little more manure or compost and a sprinkling of bonemeal.

Cultivation Runner beans are very tender and prone to frost damage and it is not really safe to sow out of doors before the end of April, even in warm areas. Mid-May is a more generally suitable time and another sowing can be made in June for a late crop. Sow the seeds singly 2 in. deep in a double row with 12 in. between the two rows of seeds and 9 to 12 in. between the seeds in the row. Successive pairs of rows should be at least 5 ft. apart. It is necessary to support the young plants, allowing one long bean pole to each. The poles in turn are secured to a cross bar at the top for additional stability. Sometimes the poles are arranged in wigwam fashion. Bean poles are not very easy to obtain nowadays but bamboo canes, netting, strings or wires are all equally suitable.

Early crops can be had by sowing under cloches or in pots or boxes in a greenhouse or frame and the seedlings hardened off for planting out in late May or early June, and this is much safer than sowing in cold soil and getting poor germination.

Water the plants freely in dry weather and spray the beans with clear water when in flower to help setting. The growing tip of each plant is pinched out when it reaches the top of the pole. Feed during early August and for this I like to use a solution of nitrate of soda (½ oz. to a gal-

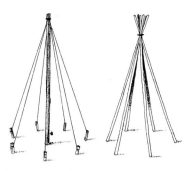

More ways of supporting runner beans

lon of water). It should be applied after watering. Pick the beans regularly as soon as they reach a usable size – this keeps them cropping – and eat them when they are young and fresh.

There are some useful dwarf varieties which do not need staking as they grow only 18 in. high. These should be spaced 12 in. apart in rows set 3 ft. apart.

It is also possible to grow the ordinary runner beans without staking by pinching out the leading runner when it is between 18 and 24 in. high and then pinching out the growing tips of all young shoots or runners, in this case the plants should be spaced 3 ft. apart each way. The resulting beans will tend to be twisted rather than straight, but the flavour is unchanged.

Varieties Streamline and Scarlet Emperor are both varieties I like and Hammond's Dwarf Scarlet is good for small gardens and early crops.
What goes wrong One of the most common setbacks to the runner bean crop is caused by the flowers dropping or failing to set. This is usually brought about by cold nights, dry soil or a combination of the two. So when deciding where to sow, choose a sheltered position, then prepare the soil well and remember to water generously throughout the season and to spray the flowers over with water to encourage setting.

Keep a watch for blackfly and spray regularly to stop them getting established.

Beetroot

sow April to July
HARVEST July to October
YIELD 8 lb. to a 10-ft. row
STORE In sand or peat in a cool shed

Beetroot is a root crop which is very easy to grow. There are three principal types – globe-rooted, long-rooted and tankard. For early crops the globe-rooted type is favourite while the other two should be considered for main crops and storing.

Position The soil should be well worked and should have been manured for a previous crop. Dress with a general fertilizer before sowing.

Cultivation Beetroot rapidly becomes coarse and to maintain a supply of young tender roots it is important to make small successional sowings at monthly intervals, beginning in April with the first sowing of a globe-rooted variety. Finish with a sowing in late June or early July to give roots for autumn and winter use.

Seeds should be sown in drills 1 in. deep and 15 in. apart. Place the seeds in clusters of two or three 6 to 8 in. apart and later thin the resulting seedlings to leave one in each position. Keep the ground well hoed and watered.

Start lifting the roots in July as they reach the size of a cricket ball – the smaller ones can be particularly tender and delicious – taking care not to bruise or damage them. This is especially important for the later maturing varieties which may be wanted for storing. Before storing cut or twist the tops from the roots, taking care not to cut too close to the crown, and put the roots in sand or light soil in a frostproof shed or other sheltered place.

Varieties Crimson Globe and Suttons' Globe give uniform crops with good dark crimson colour. Cheltenham Green Top and Housewives' Choice are long-rooted kinds.

SWISS CHARD This is the silver or seakale beet and it is grown in the same way as ordinary beetroot, the seed being sown in May, June and July for use during autumn and winter. In contrast to the ordinary beet, Swiss chard is grown for its leaves which have a dual purpose – the

Swiss chard

Young marrows forming

green part being eaten like spinach and the thick fleshy white mid-rib cooked in the same way as seakale.

What goes wrong Very little, beetroot is relatively free from attack by pests and diseases.

Broccoli

SOW March, April to May
HARVEST September to June
YIELD 12½ lb. to a 10-ft. row
STORE By freezing

Sprouting broccoli

There is no real distinction between broccoli and cauliflower but broccoli is used to describe the hardier autumn and spring kinds while cauliflower describes the more delicate summer varieties. There are two kinds of broccoli: the heading sort with close white heads and the sprouting sort which bears numerous purple-, green- or white-flowering shoots produced successively for quite a long period in spring.

Position Well-worked and firm soil, preferably one that has been manured for a previous crop. A dressing of lime is helpful in lessening the incidence of club root disease.

Cultivation Sow seeds ½ in. deep in drills placed 9 in. apart. Transplant the resulting seedlings to the beds of well-dug soil and space the plants 3 ft. apart with 3 ft. between rows. The main sowing period is in early April, but early varieties can be sown in late March and the late heading varieties in late April or early May.

During the summer hoe regularly and feed once or twice with a general fertilizer before the heads begin to form. In autumn draw a little soil around the stems to provide better anchorage. In exposed areas plants often need staking. If you are growing the heading broccoli, break some leaves over the curds as they form to protect them from frost.

Cut the curds as soon as they are well grown and before they start to open and pick the shoots of the sprouting broccoli as soon as the flower shoots are well formed and again before the flower buds open – include 5 or 6 in. of the edible portion of the stem and leaves.

Varieties Sprouting broccoli – Calabrese (September to November harvesting) good for freezing, Early Purple Sprouting (January to February), Purple Sprouting and White Sprouting (March to April). Heading broccoli – Autumn Protecting, Veitch's Self-protecting (autumn harvesting), Snow's Winter White, Superb Early White (January and February), Leamington, St. George, Satisfaction (spring harvesting), Late Queen, Whitsuntide, May Queen (May and June).

What goes wrong Watch out for attacks from the caterpillars of the cabbage white butterflies and cabbage moth, flea beetle, aphids, white fly, cabbage root fly and especially pigeons. Club root is the main disease which is likely to occur, particularly if the soil tends to be rather acid. Before planting, I think it is a good idea to dip the roots of young plants in a paste made from calomel dust and water. This will help to deter attacks of both flea beetle and club root. Dusting the seed drills with calomel dust will also act as a deterrent against these two.

Brussels Sprouts

SOW February under glass,
March out of doors
HARVEST September to February
and later
YIELD 5½ lb. to a 10-ft. row
STORE By freezing

This popular and important vegetable is one of the best of the brassicas and has the same general requirements as cabbage.

Position Good rich soil, previously manured, limed and well firmed.

Cultivation Sow the seeds in February in a frame or cool greenhouse or sow out of doors in March. Under glass the seeds may be sown in boxes; out of doors sow them thinly in drills ½ in. deep and 9 in. apart. In April and May plant the seedlings 3 ft. apart each way in well-worked firm soil. It is important not to skimp on space as close planting leads to smaller crops and sprouts of a lower quality. Lettuce, early cabbage or early cauliflower can be used as intercrops.

Water well in dry weather and feed occasionally in summer with small quantities of a general fertilizer at a rate of 1 oz. per yard run. Do not give any fertilizer after mid-August. Hoe frequently to check weeds and keep the surface soil loose, which also helps to conserve soil moisture.

The plants can get very large and may then require individual staking. In autumn draw some soil around the stems to prevent wind rock and keep removing any yellowing leaves as this helps to prevent fungal attack.

Gather the sprouts a few at a time from each plant starting from the bottom of the stems as soon as the lowest sprouts reach a usable size. Yellowing leaves can be removed at any time but do not cut off the tops of the plants until all the sprouts have been gathered, usually in February, when the tops will make a useful green vegetable.

Varieties I find that the F_1 hybrids are better than many of the older varieties as they make compact plants producing a uniform crop of solid sprouts. Thor, Leda and Peer Gynt are typical F_1 varieties. An F_1 hybrid is the result of the first cross between two distinct varieties or species and the plants produced usually show an improvement on the parents, either by increased cropping or by being of a larger size.

Other good varieties include Iceball, Cambridge Nos. 1 and 5, Fillbasket and Winter Harvest.

What goes wrong As with other brassicas the main problems come from pigeons, cabbage caterpillars, aphids, whitefly, cabbage root fly, flea beetles and club root disease. The last two can be especially devastating and routine control measures should be taken when sowing the seed or setting out young plants.

Loose-leaved or 'blown' sprouts occur on soil which is inadequately firmed or to which too much compost or manure has been added before planting. Early sowing in cold soil or in dry conditions with inadequate watering causes similar trouble.

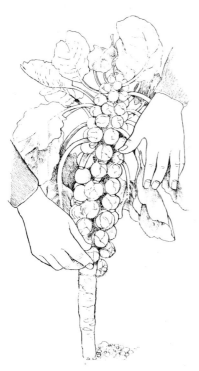

Picking brussels sprouts

Cabbage

s o w Summer heading: February under glass, March out of doors
Autumn and winter heading: March to May
Spring heading: July to August
HARVEST All year round
YIELD Spring kinds 7 lb. to a 10-ft. row
Autumn and winter 15 lb. to a 10-ft. row

There are a number of types of cabbages which make it possible to maintain a supply throughout the year. The quick-growing varieties are for summer use, slower-growing kinds for autumn use, very late and hardy kinds for use in winter. There are also kinds which can be sown in summer for cutting the following spring and, of course, the red cabbages for pickling – though these are also delicious when cooked.

All cabbages require a lot of room so if your garden is limited in area this is not a crop for you.

Position All the brassicas demand a rich, well-firmed soil and every effort should be made to prepare the ground well in advance of planting to give it time to settle. If early, short season crops have been grown, simply rake the vacated ground as this ensures that the soil has a moderate degree of solidity. Cabbages are not difficult to grow but they do take a lot out of the soil and it is advisable to make sure that they are crop rotated, this also helps to lessen the danger of diseases such as club root building up. Cabbages grow best in a soil which has been limed prior to planting at a rate of 3 oz. to the sq. yd., and this also acts as a deterrent to club root disease.

Cultivation Summer cabbages: sow seed in boxes in a frame or green-house in February, or out of doors in March in drills ½ in. deep and 9 in. apart. Plant out in April and May.

Autumn and winter cabbages: sow out of doors in March, April or early May and plant out from May to late June.

Spring cabbages: sow out of doors between mid-July and mid-August and plant out in September or October.

The best results with red cabbage are obtained by sowing the seeds in August, over-wintering the plants in a seed bed and planting out the following spring.

When planting out topdress the soil with a general fertilizer at 2 oz. per sq. yd. and space seedlings 18 in. apart in rows 2 ft. apart but allow the drumhead and red cabbage varieties a little more room, the spring varieties can do with a little less. The summer, autumn and winter kinds should be fed once in summer with a quick-acting nitrogenous fertilizer, such as Nitro-chalk or sulphate of ammonia, which should be applied as a topdressing at the rate of 2 oz. per sq. yd. and hoed in. Spring cabbage should be fed in the same way once danger of prolonged frost is passed.

Firm any plants that may have been loosened by frost action.

Varieties For summer heading – Primo, Greyhound, June Market and the F₁ hybrids May Star and June Star.

For autumn and winter heading – Winnigstadt, which is, I think, the finest of all cabbage, Christmas Drumhead, January King.

For spring heading – Harbinger, Flower of Spring, Wheeler's Imperial. Red cabbage varieties include Blood Red and Large Red Drumhead.

What goes wrong Cabbages are heavy feeders and heartless crops indicate too little organic material in the soil and a lack of firmness. If possible, make sure that compost or manure is dug in during the autumn preceeding sowing.

Once again keep a watch for the numerous pests which may be a prob-lem, namely caterpillars, cabbage root fly, aphids, flea beetle and white-fly and remember that club root disease is best defeated by adequate liming of the soil and crop rotation but routine control measures against both club root and flea beetle should be taken when sowing seed or setting out young plants.

Carrots

SOW March to July
HARVEST June onwards
YIELD Early type 3 lb. to a 10-ft. row
Main crop 7½ lb. to a 10-ft. row
STORE In sand or peat in a cool shed

This hardy and popular root crop is divided into 3 types: the short stump-rooted varieties which have cylindrical roots; intermediate medium length varieties either blunt-ended or with tapering roots and long-rooted varieties with long tapering roots. The short, stump-rooted kinds are quick maturing and therefore used for early summer cropping while the other two are best for main crops and storing during the winter. The long-rooted kinds are grown mainly for exhibition.

Position Light sandy soils are ideal and heavy soils must be improved by thorough cultivation, preferably by deep digging in autumn and winter followed by an application of a general fertilizer just before sowing at 4 oz. per sq. yd. Do not add fresh manure to the soil as this encourages the roots to fork. Sun or partial shade are equally suitable but a fully sunny place is best for early crops.

Cultivation Begin sowing seeds of the early maturing varieties out of doors in March under cloches and continue with small successional

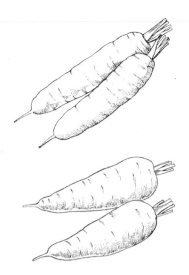

batches until mid-April. Sow thinly in drills $\frac{1}{4}$ in. deep and 8 in. apart. Sowings of main crop varieties can start out of doors in April and continue until mid-July. Once again scatter the seeds in $\frac{1}{4}$ in. deep drills but allow 12 in. between drills for the long-rooted and intermediate varieties. All kinds need only a light covering of soil and seedlings should be thinned from 4 to 8 in. apart. If you delay the final thinning until the small carrots have formed, you can eat the thinnings, which will have a sweet flavour and be very tender. In areas where the winters are not too severe stump-rooted varieties can be sown in July to provide a crop during autumn and early winter.

Keep well hoed and watch for carrot fly attack, dusting the soil with naphthalene is a good preventive measure. Main crop and intermediate varieties lifted in October can be stored in sand in a cool, frostproof shed. Cut off all top growth, except for an inch or so, before storing and do not attempt to keep any damaged roots. Lift and store before the roots start to split, which happens quickly once the autumn rains begin. *Varieties* Early – Scarlet Horn, Early Nantes, Amsterdam Forcing, Market Favourite.

Second early and main crop – James Scarlet Intermediate, Autumn King, Chantenay Red Cored and Long Red St. Valery.

What goes wrong Carrot fly is the major problem and in a serious attack the roots can become worthless through depredations of the grubs.

Forking of the roots can be caused by manure in the soil – always grow in soil which has been manured for a previous crop and which has been dug as deeply as possible. Splitting occurs most frequently when a wet autumn follows a dry summer but too much nitrogen can be a contributory factor.

Cauliflower

SOW February to April and September
HARVEST July to November
YIELD 10 lb. to a 10-ft. row
STORE By freezing

The author spreading some fine specimens of onions to dry in a frame. The heating cables around the sides of the frame extend its uses in cold weather

Cauliflowers are very similar in appearance to the heading broccoli (page 43) but more tender and with a rather more delicate flavour. The curds are formed from the unopened flowers.

Position This is a crop which must be grown quickly in good, well-firmed well-manured soil. A sunny but sheltered situation is best.

Cultivation Start sowing seed in February in boxes in a frame or greenhouse. Do not try to make outdoor sowings until early April. An outdoor sowing can also be made in early September, from which the seedlings can be transplanted at the end of October to a frame where they will spend the winter. They are planted outside in April for an early crop.

Plants from the late winter and early spring sowings should be pricked out as soon as the seed leaves (the first leaves) are formed and hardened off for planting out in May or early June. Ideally, they should be planted as soon as the second or third leaves are formed, if left in their boxes they will become starved and when they are eventually planted they will form only small curds. So the smaller the plants are when they are planted out the more likely they are to produce large curds.

Plant 2 ft. apart in rows $2\frac{1}{2}$ ft. apart, water well in dry weather and feed occasionally with a general fertilizer at a rate of 2 oz. per sq. yd. Firm well after planting, check and re-firm the plants after strong winds and, in exposed areas, stake the plants if necessary. Hoe frequently to control weeds and conserve moisture in the soil.

As the curds develop break some of the inner leaves over them to keep

47

Protecting a cauliflower curd

them white and cut as soon as they are well grown. One indication of ripeness is that the separate sections of the curd are easily distinguishable.

Varieties For autumn and winter sowing – All the Year Round, Early Snowball, Cambridge No. 5.

For spring sowing – Veitch's Autumn Giant, Conquest, White Heart and I find that the Australian varieties are very good, try Boomerang and Kangaroo.

What goes wrong Another member of the popular brassica group, cauliflowers are subject to attack from the same pests and diseases as their relatives, see under broccoli. However, summer cauliflowers are especially prone to attacks from cabbage root fly and flea beetle and I use routine control measures against these pests.

Other problems can arise from lack of good cultivation techniques and if you have trouble with the plants bolting, and by this I mean the curds running up to seed, and poor curd production then it often means that the soil was not firm enough before the plants were put in. Heartless crops can also indicate a lack of organic matter in the soil which, in turn, affects the soil moisture content. It is important that cauliflowers should suffer no check to growth from lack of water, so do not plant in hot, dry weather and, as cauliflowers have a tendency to go 'blind', examine all young plants before planting to make sure that each has a growing point.

Celeriac

SOW March to April
HARVEST September to March
STORE In a cool shed in sand or peat
YIELD 10 lb. to a 10-ft. row

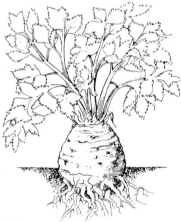

Celery

SOW Late February to early April
HARVEST September to January
YIELD 14 lb. to a 10-ft. row

This is a close relative of celery which it resembles in flavour and it is a useful vegetable for growing on poorer drier soil than is tolerated by celery. The bulbous root crowns are the edible portion and these can be cooked whole, used to flavour soups and stews or shredded in salads.

Position Soil which has been well dug and manured and an open situation.

Cultivation Sow the seeds in a cool greenhouse or frame in March or April and harden off the seedlings for planting out of doors in May, 1 ft. apart in rows 1½ ft. apart. No earthing up is needed and the only subsequent attention required is regular hoeing and generous watering in summer. Remove any side growths that appear because if these are allowed to grow they will spoil the shape of the roots.

You can start to harvest the roots in late summer. In warmer parts of the country roots can be left in the ground for the winter, covered with bracken and straw and dug out as required. Elsewhere, lift all roots before the frost arrives and store in sand in an airy shed.

Varieties Globus is a good variety.

What goes wrong Although celeriac is subject to attack from the same pests and diseases as celery, it is unlikely that any will be severe.

There are three types of celery: white, pink or red, and self-blanching. The self-blanching is suitable for summer and early autumn use, this is followed by the white celery and then the pink or red, which is the hardiest and can be used later than the other two types, into December and January.

Position The soil must be deeply dug and well manured as celery is both a heavy feeder and heavy drinker.

Cultivation The seeds are small and germinate slowly so it is better to raise the young plants under glass. Sow the seeds in a warm greenhouse at the end of February for an early crop and in March or early April for a later supply. The seedlings must be pricked off into deep boxes and hardened off for planting out in May or early June.

If you are going to grow the white, pink or red types, dig a trench 1 to 1½ ft. deep and as much across and then mix garden compost or well-rotted manure with some of the excavated soil and return this to the trench. The top 5 or 6 in. of the trench is not refilled and the surplus soil is built into ridges on either side of the trench, for later use in earthing up. Sprinkle a dressing of general fertilizer along the trench at the rate of 1½ oz. to the yard run and lightly fork this in. The plants should be set 1 ft. apart in a single row down the centre of the trench. The trenches should be 3 ft. apart.

The self-blanching type does not need to be planted in a trench as there is no need for any earthing up. Set the plants out in blocks, 9 in. apart in each direction. In this way the foliage provides cover for the stems.

During the growing season celery needs a lot of water, it is almost impossible to over-water, and regular feeding with weak liquid manure or a general fertilizer once the plants are established.

In early August, you should start to blanch the celery (the white and pink or red kinds). First remove any small offsets, then wrap lengths of newspaper around the stems, securing them loosely with raffia, but allowing room for the hearts to develop. This stops soil from getting into the hearts when it is drawn up around the plants. Approximately six to eight weeks is required for blanching and the idea is to add more soil at weekly intervals until only the top tuft of leaves is left exposed. In autumn and winter it is necessary to protect the exposed tops with straw or bracken.

Celery takes up quite a lot of space and during the early summer months catch crops such as lettuces and radish can be grown on the ridges between trenches.

Varieties Golden Self-blanching, Solid White (one of the best in my opinion), Giant White, Superb Pink, Giant Red.

What goes wrong Watch out for celery fly, as this can become troublesome if prompt action is not taken. Brown spots on the leaves are indicative of leaf spot. This is a fungal disease which can spread rapidly if not checked, particularly in a wet season. Many seedsmen are now offering celery seed which has been treated to prevent leaf spot disease developing but additional precautions may still be necessary.

Soils containing an excess of nitrogen can lead to the development of a rot in the centre of the plants. Known as heart rot or soft rot the bacterium responsible usually gains entry through wounds or is transmitted by celery fly larvae or slugs. The use of balanced fertilizers and eradication of pests will give a measure of control. Take care, too, when earthing up not to damage the stems.

Celery which runs up to seed is usually caused by the plants receiving a check from lack of water in dry weather or by the young plants remaining in the seed boxes for too long before being planted out.

Blanching celery

Chicory

SOW May or June
HARVEST Throughout the winter

This vegetable is grown for its tightly packed hearts of leaves or 'chicons' which are blanched and eaten either cooked or raw. They are crisp, creamy white and make a good alternative to salads when these are scarce and expensive in winter.

Position Well dug soil manured for a previous crop.

Cultivation Sow the seeds in May or early June in drills $\frac{1}{2}$ in. deep and 15 in. apart in good well-drained soil and then thin the resulting seedlings to 1 ft. apart. During the summer the object is to build up good roots, so any flowering shoots are removed as they appear. In November cut off all the leaves about 1 in. above the crowns and lift these carefully. You will find that the roots will be about 3 in. thick at the top and probably 12 in. in length. Trim them back to 8 in. and store them in a cool, frostproof shed for forcing, a few at a time, to provide a succession of chicons throughout the winter.

To force, place the roots close together and right way up in deep boxes or large pots and pack with fairly moist old potting or seed compost. Five can be accommodated in a 9-in. pot. As forcing must be done in the dark, invert another container of the same size over the pot or box containing the plants and keep them in a temperature of 10 to 13°C. (50 to 55°F.). Cellars, sheds or under the staging of a greenhouse are all suitable places, provided the temperature is correct. The process of forcing and blanching takes about three weeks.

Out of doors chicory can be blanched in situ by covering each plant with a flower pot or by drawing soil up into a ridge as for earthing up celery. The forced roots are of no further use.

Whether grown indoors or out, the blanched growths of young leaves (chicons) are cut off close to the crown when they are about 9 in. high.

Varieties Large Brussels, Witloof.

What goes wrong Chicory seems to be largely unaffected by any troubles.

Cress

SOW April to August out of doors
September to March with protection
HARVEST All the year round

An excellent salad vegetable particularly useful during the winter and one of the components of the ever-popular mustard and cress, which is such a good crop for children to grow.

Cultivation You can sow the seeds broadcast in the open ground from

April to the end of August and indoors or under glass during the rest of the year. The only requirement is that a temperature of about 13°C. (55°F.) can be maintained.

Indoor sowings are most successful made in shallow boxes on damp sacking, blotting paper or flannel. Alternatively, you can use peat or soil. Sow evenly and fairly thickly. Do not cover the seeds with soil, a sheet of paper placed over the box will be sufficient until germination occurs, when it must be removed. Water when necessary with slightly warm water. Cut when the seedlings are 2 to 3 in. in height.

As cress takes longer to grow than mustard, sow the former three days before the latter if they are wanted for cutting at the same time.

Varieties Extra Fine Curled, Super Salad and the American or Land Cress. The latter resembles watercress but can be grown in ordinary soil.

What goes wrong As the cress is eaten in the seedling stage the only problem is likely to be caused by damping off. To prevent this, keep the atmosphere cool and dry and if soil is used as a growing medium make sure it has been sterilized.

Cucumber

SOW January to May under glass (Frame type)
May out of doors (Ridge type)
HARVEST July to September
YIELD 10 lb. to a 10-ft. row

There are two main types of cucumber: the ridge, for growing out of doors and the frame, for growing in greenhouses or frames.

Cultivation of frame cucumbers From January until late April sow the seeds in twos in 3-in. pots of John Innes seed compost and germinate in a temperature of 18°C. (65°F.). After germination thin to leave one seedling in each pot.

In greenhouses, the planting beds can be prepared either on the floor or on a flat staging, depending on the greenhouse height. The growing medium should be a rich compost made up of fibrous loam, leafmould and well-rotted manure. A ridge of this compost about 15 in. wide and 7 in. deep in the centre is sufficient for young plants, but whenever roots appear on the surface they should be covered with a layer of similar compost. Make up the bed at least one week before planting to allow time for it to become thoroughly warm. Set the plants out at intervals of 3 to 5 ft., planting each on a slight mound as this will help to prevent water collecting around the base of the stem and possibly causing stem rot. Strain wires lengthwise along the house at distances of 15 in. to support the growths.

With cucumbers a certain amount of training is required: allow the main growths to run up until they reach the apex of the roof and then take out the tips. Train side growths horizontally along the wires and pinch out the shoot tips at the second leaf joint.

Cucumbers need fairly careful watering – they must not be allowed to dry out but on the other hand must not be waterlogged. Spray the plants daily with tepid water and make sure that some form of shading from strong sunshine is used. When the flowers appear, remove all the male ones as it is undesirable that the female flowers should be pollinated since this results in bitter tasting fruit. A female flower can be distinguished by the tiny immature cucumber visible at the back of the flower. Male flowers have thin straight stalks.

Applications of liquid manure should be given as soon as the first fruits begin to develop and these should be continued weekly. Ventilate the house in hot weather, preferably from the top.

Pinching out a shoot tip at the second leaf joint

In frames, make a mound in the centre of each of the same compost used in greenhouses or John Innes No. 3 compost and set one plant to each frame. Do not plant too deeply. Pinch out the growing point of each plant when it has produced about six leaves. Allow four of the resulting side shoots to develop and spread them evenly to the four corners of the frame, pegging them to the soil. Stop each of these shoots when it has formed two leaves. Once again remove all male flowers to prevent pollination. Water liberally and spray the plants with water. Feed with liquid fertilizer as described previously and topdress with more compost when white roots show on the surface of the soil. Shade the glass to prevent sunscorch. As the young cucumbers begin to form, place a slate or a piece of glass or wood underneath each to keep them off the soil.

Cultivation of ridge cucumbers Choose a sunny sheltered position and build up a ridge of good soil and well-rotted manure or compost.

In mid-April, sow seeds in twos in 3-in. pots of seed compost and keep the pots in a frame or greenhouse until germination. Thin to one seedling in each pot. Harden the plants off and plant out, 3 to 4 ft. apart, in the ridges of soil in late May. If you plant in early May it will be necessary to give some cloche protection. The seeds of ridge cucumbers can also be sown out of doors in the open ground in the middle of May but earlier fruits will be obtained from the indoor sowings.

Pinch out the tip of each plant when it has made about six leaves. As the side shoots grow train them evenly around the plants and peg them to the soil. Water freely and feed once a week with weak liquid manure from the time that the first fruits begin to swell. With ridge cucumbers it is important that the female flowers are pollinated with pollen from the male flowers so do not remove these. As previously described protect each developing cucumber by placing a slate or piece of wood or glass under it.

Cut cucumbers regularly as soon as they reach usable size.

Varieties Frame – Improved Telegraph, Butcher's Disease Resisting. The new all-female varieties like Femspot and Femina are useful and save the work of removing male flowers though I do not think the flavour is as good as some of the others.

Ridge – Burpee Hybrid, Prolific Ridge, Nadir, Gherkin (for pickling).

What goes wrong Look out for mildew and stem rot, though the latter should not be troublesome if care is given to watering. Whitefly and

Ridge cucumber

aphids may be a problem and under glass red spider mite will most likely attack plants if a damp atmosphere is not maintained. Mosaic virus diseases may be seen and affected plants should be burned.

Endive

SOW April to August
HARVEST August to March
YIELD 8 heads to a 10-ft. row

Endive looks rather like a curly leaved lettuce but it is, in fact, a member of the chicory family. It is grown for use in salads and has the advantage of hardiness, which makes it possible to obtain crops during the winter.
Position Rich, well-dug soil and an open situation. Apply a dressing of superphosphate at 1 oz. per sq. yd. just before sowing.
Cultivation Seeds are sown thinly in ½-in. deep drills 1 ft. apart at intervals from April to August and the seedlings are thinned to 9 in. apart. When the plants are well grown you should cover each one with an inverted flower pot, making sure that the hole in the bottom is in turn covered with a piece of wood or a plate. This will exclude light and ensure that the leaves are blanched – a process taking six weeks, and resulting in an improved flavour.

This crop should be grown quickly and during the summer it is a good idea to give a couple of topdressings of nitrate of soda, Nitro-chalk or sulphate of ammonia at 1 oz. to 12 ft.

The later sown endive can be protected with a frame or cloches in the autumn and in this case a sufficient degree of blanching can be obtained by covering the glass with black polythene for the last few weeks before harvesting.
Varieties Moss Curled, Green Curled, Exquisite Curled.

Blanching endive. A saucer can be used to blanch the centre leaves only

Kale (Borecole)

SOW April to May
HARVEST November to May
YIELD 15 lb. to a 10-ft. row

There is a group of vegetables covered by this heading, some grown for their leaves, others for their young shoots. Many of the varieties have curled plume-like leaves, some dark green while others have a purplish cast. Kale is yet another member of the brassicas.
Position and *Cultivation* Soil and cultivation is in most respects as described for sprouting broccoli. However, seed is sown slightly later, in April and May, and the young plants are transplanted 18 in. apart in rows 2½ ft. apart in July and August.

Kale can be harvested on a 'cut-and-come-again' method, by cutting the outer leaves as they mature.
Varieties Extra Curled Scotch, Hungry Gap.
What goes wrong Pests, diseases and other problems are the same as for cabbage.

Kohl-rabi

sow April to August
HARVEST July to November
YIELD 7lb. to a 10-ft. row
STORE In a cool shed in sand or
peat

Kohl-rabi is an excellent vegetable, popular on the Continent but not yet well known here. The bulb-like stems are the edible portion, they have a rather turnip-like taste and should be harvested when they are the size of tennis balls. They can be eaten cooked like turnips or sliced raw in salads.

Position Good soil, if possible manured for a previous crop, well dug and dressed with superphosphate at 3 oz. per sq. yd. and sulphate of potash at ½ oz. per sq. yd.

Cultivation The seeds are sown thinly in drills ½ in. deep and 15 in. apart and the resulting seedlings thinned to leave 9 in. between them. Sowings can be made in succession from late April until August if you wish to even out the supply.

Water and hoe regularly and give several feeds with a general fertilizer to keep the plants growing rapidly.

Kohl-rabi can be stored for a short time in sand or peat in a garden shed.

Varieties Early Purple, Early White.

What goes wrong Kohl-rabi is relatively free from troubles but aphids may be seen.

Leeks

sow March out of doors
January or February under glass
HARVEST September to May
YIELD 12 plants to a 10-ft. row

Planting out leeks

Leeks are a useful winter crop which does, however, make heavy demands on the soil.

Position A rich, well-manured soil. Before sowing topdress with a general fertilizer.

Cultivation For an early crop and for exhibition purposes seeds should be sown in boxes in a warm greenhouse in January or February. Out of doors delay sowing until late March and then set the seeds thinly in rows 1 ft. apart. The seedlings raised under glass will need to be pricked out into boxes (or singly into small pots if required for exhibition) as soon as they can be handled and then gradually hardened off for planting out in May. The outdoor-sown leeks are usually transplanted in June. In both cases the plants should be 8 or 9 in. apart in rows 18 in. apart.

During the summer, hoe frequently and water well in dry weather. In June and July feed every 10 days or so with weak liquid manure or with a general fertilizer. As the young plants grow the stems must be earthed up to ensure blanching.

The method of planting just described is the one to use if you are growing leeks for exhibition. If not, the young plants can be placed in 6- to 8-in. deep holes (9 in. apart) made with a thick dibber. Drop a plant into each hole so that only the leaf tips show above the rim but do not refill the holes with soil, just water the plants in thoroughly. The rows should be set 1 ft. apart. A third method, suitable for raising small leeks, is to thin the outdoor-sown seedlings in the seed bed and then gradually draw up soil around them to blanch the stems.

Leeks are quite hardy and can be left in the ground over winter to be lifted and used as required. However, if you wish to prepare the ground for other crops then the remaining plants can be lifted and heeled in in a cool sheltered part of the garden.

Varieties Musselburgh, Prizetaker.

What goes wrong Although leeks belong to the same family as onions and can be attacked by the same range of pests and diseases, in fact these create few problems.

Lettuce

SOW February to October
HARVEST June to October, main crop
Early spring with protection
YIELD 10 to 13 heads to a 10-ft. row

Types of lettuce

There are two main types of lettuce, the cabbage and the cos, and a large number of varieties of each varying in colour, size, season and texture.

Position Rich, well-manured and well-prepared soil will encourage the quick growth essential for this crop. A sunny situation is best.

Cultivation For early crops sow seeds in pots or boxes of sandy soil in a greenhouse in late February. The seedlings should be pricked out as soon as they can be handled and then hardened off thoroughly prior to planting out in a sheltered spot under cloches in late March or early April.

Outdoor sowings can be made a little at a time at fortnightly intervals from March until mid-August, provided cloche protection is given to the earliest of these. Sow thinly in ½-in. deep drills, 12 in. apart. Thin the seedlings to 12 in. apart for the bigger varieties and 9 in. for the smaller ones such as Tom Thumb. The thinnings can be transplanted to give a slightly later supply, see page 23.

Be generous with watering in hot weather as it is important to grow lettuces fast and without a check. In poor soil and warm conditions lettuces make slow growth and run to seed quickly.

Lettuces are very useful as a catch crop, sowings being made on the ridges of celery trenches or between rows of peas.

Some hardy varieties are available for sowing out of doors in late August or early September for cropping in early spring. Sow as before in drills and plant the seedlings 9 in. apart in rows 12 in. apart in early October. Choose a warm, sheltered border and put slug pellets down the rows in late autumn and early spring. By covering some of the plants with cloches you will be able to advance maturity a little more. In March, feed winter lettuces with a general fertilizer, at a rate of 2 oz. to each sq. yd., sprinkled beside the rows and hoed in. Take care to keep it off the leaves.

Other varieties can be sown in the autumn for winter cultivation in a greenhouse or frame. All lettuces grown under glass should be planted shallowly as damping off may occur if the lowest leaves are not above soil level.

Varieties Summer cabbage type (spring and summer sowing) – All the Year Round, Webb's Wonderful, Tom Thumb, Unrivalled, Continuity.

Winter cabbage type (autumn sowing for early spring cropping) – Imperial Winter, Arctic King.

Forcing lettuces (autumn sowing in greenhouses for winter and early spring cropping) – Kordaat, Cheshunt Early Giant, May Queen.

Cos type – Lobjoits Green, Little Gem, Winter Density. The latter is really intermediate between cabbage and cos types and can be used as a summer or winter variety.

What goes wrong Watch out for signs of mildew and botrytis because if the conditions are right these fungi will spread rapidly.

Aphids and slugs can be a problem and also cutworms. The latter are greyish caterpillars which attack the plants at or below the soil level, often cutting right through the neck. They can be especially troublesome on winter crops. Control by hoeing lindane or naphthalene into the soil.

Lettuce usually bolt rapidly once they reach maturity so do remember the importance of sowing little and often to avoid a glut. Heartless crops indicate a lack of organic matter in the soil.

Marrow

SOW April under glass
May out of doors
YIELD Varies with the type
STORE In a frostproof shed

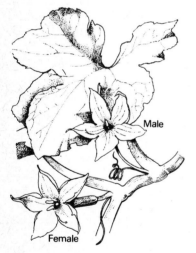

Marrow flowers

There are several kinds of marrow: the bush type (the best for average sized gardens) of which Courgette is probably the most popular variety; the trailing type, producing the familiar long, striped fruit and the unusual custard marrows with pumpkin-shaped fruits of delicious flavour.

Position Rich loamy soil or old turves mixed with a little well-rotted manure make the best growing medium. Either build the compost into a heap or excavate a trench 2 ft. wide and 2 ft. deep and fill this with the compost but leaving the surface a little below the ground level so that the plants can be flooded with water in dry weather. The old technique of growing these vegetables was to plant them on a heap of compost or manure because the best results are obtained by growing them on a good moisture-retaining medium.

Cultivation Sow the seeds in twos in 3-in pots during April and germinate in a temperature of 18°C. (65°F.). Thin the seedlings to leave the best one in each pot as soon as they can be handled easily. It is possible to sow out of doors where the plants are to grow but do not attempt this before mid-May and then cover the seeds with cloches or jam jars until germination has taken place.

Plant in early June, setting bush varieties 3 ft. apart, and trailing ones 4 ft. apart. If possible, cover with cloches for the first week after planting. Pinch the ends of the runners of the trailing varieties when they have reached a length of about 3 ft. This will encourage the production of side shoots which usually carry the female flowers. If too many side shoots grow they can be reduced by thinning. The Courgette and other bush marrows require no such pinching or thinning.

Pollinate the female flowers, which can be recognized by the slight swelling just beneath them, by picking the male flowers and inverting these over the female.

Water freely at all times and feed with weak liquid manure as soon as the first marrows start to swell. Harvest while still young and tender before the outer skins harden. At the end of the season cut any remaining ripe fruits and store in a frostproof place, a good way is to hang them in nets or string bags so that the air can circulate freely around them.

Varieties Bush Type – White Bush, Green Bush, Courgette and Tender and True. The last is a round green marrow which ripens to a bright yellow. Also falling in the bush group are the custard marrows. These have unusual white or yellow flattish fruits which have a scalloped edge.

Trailing type – Long White, Long Green, Table Dainty and the unusual Vegetable Spaghetti, which is so named because after being boiled whole the inside comes away like spaghetti.

What goes wrong The main diseases are grey mould, especially troublesome in wet seasons, mildew and mosaic. The latter is a virus disease which is recognized by yellow blotches or mottling on the leaves and the fruits do not develop properly. It is best to destroy the infected plants.

The insect pests are aphids and slugs.

Melons

sow January to May
HARVEST August to September
YIELD 4 or 5 fruits to each plant

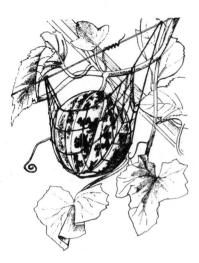

Melons supported in nets

Melons growing in a frame

Melons are exciting to grow and the flavour of a home-grown specimen so far exceeds that of a bought one that I am surprised they are not a more popular crop with gardeners. Strictly speaking they are fruits, but then so are such vegetables as tomatoes, marrows and cucumbers, and as their culture much resembles that of cucumbers and marrows I have decided to include them in this book.

Position Melons must be grown throughout in greenhouses or frames as they are not hardy enough for outdoor culture. The ideal compost should be a mixture of fibrous loam with peat and well-rotted manure but John Innes No. 3 compost is also suitable.

Cultivation In greenhouses, the seeds can be sown singly in small pots of John Innes seed compost any time from January to the end of May but I would recommend that you wait until April before making a sowing. Germinate in a temperature of 18 to 21°C. (65 to 70°F.) and plant out before the seedlings become pot bound. The plants are grown on in beds of soil either on the floor or staging, depending on the height of the greenhouse. First cover the area with a piece of plastic sheeting and then build up the bed 6 in. deep and 2½ to 3 ft. wide. A further ridge of soil, again 6 in. deep, should be built up at the back of the bed and on this the plants will be set 3 ft. apart. Take care not to plant too deeply, the first leaves must be well clear of the soil.

The plants should be trained as single stems and secured to wires strained from one end of the house to the other, 6 in. away from the roof glass. When each plant reaches the apex of the greenhouse pinch out the top. Allow 6 or more laterals to develop on each plant and stop these beyond the second leaf. On each of these laterals female flowers will form and these can be distinguished from the male flowers by a slight swelling immediately behind the petals. It is essential that the female flowers are pollinated with pollen from the male flowers. Four or five fruits to each plant are usually sufficient so other fruits must be removed before they start to develop. The pollination can be done at midday when the pollen is dry, pick the male flowers, remove some of the petals and run the stamens inside the female flowers.

Feed with liquid or soluble fertilizer from the time the young fruits start to swell and topdress the beds with well-decayed compost or manure when surface roots appear. Water freely at all times until the melons are nearly ripe and keep the atmosphere moist. However, watering should be drastically reduced once the melons begin to ripen – you can tell this by the characteristic aroma which they give off at this stage – or the fruits will split. Some shading may be necessary to prevent leaves scorching but sun is necessary to ripen the melons.

As the fruits develop and become heavy they must be supported with special melon nets or raffia bags which can be slung to the wires.

For growing in frames, sow seed in April or May and set the plants out in early June. Two plants in a frame 6 ft. by 4 ft. is usually sufficient and they should be planted in John Innes No. 3 compost. Stop the plants at the sixth rough leaf and retain six side growths for flowering and fruiting. Train these laterals outwards towards the sides of the frame and peg them to the soil. In other respects cultivation is the same as in greenhouses, except that the fruits develop at ground level and a piece of glass or slate placed under each will lift it and assist ripening. Growing the plants over soil-warming cables or in a raised bed made by mounding up the compost is an advantage.

Varieties There are numerous varieties, the white-fleshed Hero of Lockinge is suited to both greenhouses and frames. The cantaloupe variety Dutch Net is especially suited to frame cultivation as are all the cantaloupe type. Try also the F_1 hybrid Sweetheart, which in my opinion is the easiest of all. Other good varieties for the greenhouse include Emerald Gem and Superlative.

What goes wrong Red spider mite is the melon's chief enemy but it is less likely to become troublesome if a humid atmosphere is maintained. Watch out for slugs, snails and mice which may attack frame-grown fruit.

Mustard

SOW April to August out of doors
October to March under glass
HARVEST All the year round

Mustard is usually eaten in the seedling stage as an accompaniment to cress to which it adds a sharpness in flavour.

Cultivation Out of doors, seeds can be sown broadcast on finely broken soil at intervals from early April to late August. Cover with a light sprinkling of soil or mats or boards until germination takes place.

Under glass and indoors, sowings should be made thickly and evenly on the surface of shallow boxes of light, moist soil or on damp sacking, blotting paper or flannel. Cover with a sheet of paper until the seeds germinate. A temperature of about 13°C. (55°F.) is necessary.

Cut the mustard just above soil level when the seedlings are between 2 and 3 in. long. It is ready more quickly than cress and should be sown three days after cress if the two crops are required at the same time.

Varieties Finest White.

What goes wrong Damping off disease is likely to be the only problem. To prevent this use sterilized soil when growing indoors and keep the atmosphere airy and not too moist.

Onion

SOW December or January under glass
March, August and September out of doors
PLANT March or April
HARVEST June onwards
YIELD 6 lb. to a 10-ft. row
STORE In a frostproof shed

Position The soil should be rich, well worked and crumbly and the site open and sunny. Prepare the bed in the winter by digging and incorporating manure or, if you cannot obtain this, garden compost or peat. In January I like to fork bonfire ash into the soil and add a dressing of bonemeal at the rate of 2 to 4 oz. per sq. yd.

Cultivation You can begin to sow onion seed out of doors in March and with onions especially it is important that the seed beds should be well prepared. Rake the soil to a fine tilth, firm by treading and mix in a general fertilizer at about one handful to every sq. yd. Then give a final raking and sow the seeds thinly in $\frac{1}{2}$-in. deep drills set 1 ft. apart.

Under glass, seeds can be sown in boxes in late December or January in a temperature of 13 to 16°C. (55 to 60°F.). The seedlings are pricked out when they are $1\frac{1}{2}$ in. tall and later transferred singly to small pots. In these they should be hardened off for planting out in mid-April. This method produces good sized onions.

A late sowing can be made in late August or early September in a sheltered nursery bed out of doors. The seedlings are left unthinned throughout the winter and transplanted in March.

In all cases thin the tiny bulbs to 6 in. apart in rows unless required for exhibition when a little more space should be allowed.

The thinnings can be used for salads but I also like to make some sowings of a special variety for this purpose. Sowings from March onwards will provide a succession of salad onions from June and an August sowing which is not transplanted until spring will give 'spring' onions in the early part of the year. Salad onions should be sown rather more thickly than the bulb onions.

An alternative to seed sowing is to plant onion sets (tiny bulbs) in March or April. Prepare the soil well as described for seed sowing and plant the sets just below the surface 6 in. apart in rows set 1 ft. apart.

Hoe regularly during the summer, water freely when required, never allowing the soil to dry out completely, and feed every 10 days with either liquid manure or a general fertilizer. If any flower heads start to form, break or crush the stems and when growth begins to slacken in summer bend over the tops if this does not happen naturally. This will facilitate ripening. Lift the bulbs with a fork when they are fully developed and lay them out to dry in the sun, preferably where they can be protected from rain. A good way is to space them in a well-ventilated frame and then cover this with a light, so that they get all the sunshine available but are protected from rain. When the bulbs are ripe, store them in a cool airy frostproof place in ropes or bundles or on slatted shelves. It is important to store only firm bulbs which have been allowed to dry for two to three weeks.

The tree onion is a novelty which I grow in my garden. It is an unusual plant which carries clusters of small, strongly flavoured bulbs on the top of a fairly tall stem. Plant in April and increase by planting the small aerial bulbs or dividing the bulbs which form in the ground.

Yet another novelty is the Welsh onion. This is a perennial which forms thickened bases to the leaves instead of bulbs and these are useful for pulling over a long period to use in place of spring onions or chives. Sow in February to May and lift and divide every third year.

Varieties For spring sowing – Bedfordshire Champion, James Keeping. Ailsa Craig is particularly good for sowing under glass.

For autumn sowing – Autumn Queen, Solidity.

For spring onions – White Lisbon.

For pickling – The Queen, Paris Silver-skin. See also shallots page 67. Stuttgarter Giant is a good variety for onion sets, these are useful for growing in areas where onions do not succeed well from seed.

What goes wrong The chief insect pests are eelworm and onion fly, the latter often causing considerable damage. Watch out for the first signs of attack which result in the leaves turning yellow and wilting and take prompt action.

Mildew, neck rot, and white rot are the diseases most likely to be seen. White rot is caused by a soil-borne fungus which causes the leaves to yellow and the roots to rot. The best way of overcoming it is by crop rotation but a measure of control is obtained by dusting 4 per cent. calomel dust or sulphur along the drills before sowing or by dipping the sets in calomel paste.

Some gardeners have trouble with onions bolting – going to seed before they are large enough to harvest. This can be caused by planting or sowing too early in the year when periods of cold weather can effectively check growth, which in turn starts the flowering process. The best way of overcoming this in the following year is to delay planting or sowing by a fortnight.

Onions ripening

Parsnip

sow March to May
HARVEST September onwards
YIELD 8 lb. to a 10-ft. row
STORE In sand or peat in a cool
shed or leave in the ground

Parsnips are a good winter vegetable with a rather sweet pungent flavour which may not be to everyone's liking but they make an excellent addition to soups and stews.

Position A good, deeply worked soil, not freshly manured. Before sowing apply a general fertilizer at the rate of 4 oz. per sq. yd.

Cultivation The seeds are sown in March, April or early May in drills 1 in. deep and 18 in. apart. Place the seeds, two or three at a time, 9 in. apart and later thin the resulting seedlings to leave one in each cluster. If they are intended for exhibition allow rather more space.

If the soil is very stony or heavy then one way of growing parsnips successfully is to bore holes, 18 to 24 in. deep, with a crow bar and fill each with a mixture of soil with a little peat, sand and bonemeal. Then sow the seeds on top of each prepared hole.

Parsnips are a hardy crop which can be left in the ground throughout the winter for the roots improve in taste with exposure to frost. However, as the ground may freeze and make it impossible to lift them in really hard weather, I like to lift some in November and store them in sand or peat in a shed or sheltered place out of doors.

Varieties I prefer to grow Tender and True and Hollow Crown.

What goes wrong A disease which causes rotting of the roots and is known as canker is the most troublesome problem, the more so because it has a number of causes. The infection may initially be caused through injury by carrot fly or the roots cracking due to the action of rain after a spell of dry weather. An excess of nitrogen can also have a contributory effect. Control of carrot fly should not be neglected.

Forking of the roots is caused by growing the parsnips in freshly manured or very stony soil.

Peas

sow January to February under
glass
March to June and in October
outside
HARVEST June to October
YIELD 4 lb. to a 10-ft. row
STORE By freezing

There are many varieties of peas and these may be classified in various ways, primarily as early, second early and main crop, which in turn are divided into dwarf, medium and tall, and round-seeded or wrinkled-seeded types. The round-seeded peas are hardier and can be sown early but the flavour of the wrinkled-seeded (marrowfat) peas is sweeter and I like to sow a greater proportion of these.

Position A rich, well-manured, well-dug soil which has been well prepared during autumn and winter. Dress with a general fertilizer about one week before sowing.

Cultivation In a greenhouse or frame the first sowings can be made in late January or February. For this sowing I use wrinkled-seeded varieties such as Kelvedon Wonder and Little Marvel, placing five seeds in a $3\frac{1}{2}$-in. pot of John Innes No. 1 compost. After germination, they are hardened off for planting out of doors in late March or April when they may need cloche protection if the weather is cold.

If the soil and weather permit, the first outdoor sowings of round-seeded peas should be made in March, although with cloche protection sowing is possible in February. Outdoor sowings of wrinkled-seeded peas should be delayed until early April. Subsequently, sowings of main crop varieties may be continued at intervals of about a fortnight until late June. Finish with a sowing of an early variety, such as Kelvedon Wonder, in late June to provide a late crop. With peas it is important to provide a succession of cropping by sowing little and often.

A late sowing of round-seeded peas can be made out of doors at the

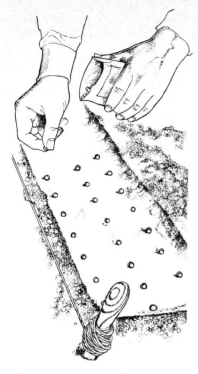

Sowing peas in a trench

end of October to provide an early crop the following spring. Sow in trenches as previously described and provide cloche protection, if possible, through the winter.

Seeds may either be sown in drills 1½ to 2 in. deep or, and this is the way I prefer to do it, in shallow, flat-bottomed trenches 8 in. wide and again about 2 in. deep, which have been taken out with a spade. Sow three rows of seeds in each trench. Space the seeds 3 to 4 in. apart.

Successive rows of peas should be spaced roughly in relation to the eventual height of the peas, 2-ft. tall peas in rows 2 ft. apart, 4-ft. peas in rows set 4 ft. apart and so on. The wider spaces between the rows can be used for quick maturing intercrops such as radish, lettuce or spinach.

Hoe regularly and water well and thoroughly when the weather is dry. Provide support (pea sticks, hazel branches or the long lasting plastic netting) for the medium and tall varieties as soon as the tendrils start to form. Dwarf varieties need not be supported but I think they are better for a few short, bushy sticks.

Picking should be done as the pods fill up and from the bottom of the plants upwards. Early peas take about 12 weeks from sowing to maturity, second early peas 14 weeks, main crop 16 weeks or more.

Varieties Early, round-seeded – Meteor, Feltham First. Both useful for early sowing under cloches and out of doors and for a November sowing. Early wrinkled-seeded – Kelvedon Wonder and Little Marvel, for sowing under glass and to provide the first outdoor sowing of this type.

Second early and main crop, wrinkled-seeded – Onward is one of the best varieties in this group. Senator and Droitwich Wonder are also good.

Sugar peas, sometimes known as Mange-tout, are a type of pea in which the pods are picked and cooked whole. They can be sown from March to June in succession and make a pleasant change from the more traditional sorts.

What goes wrong By far the most serious pest is the pea moth. The adult moth lays its eggs on the upper leaves of the plants and the resulting maggots hatch and burrow into the pea pods where they feed on the developing peas. The best time to spray is when the plants are in flower and if you apply the chemicals in the evening then you will not harm any bees which are likely to be around at this time. Insecticides containing menazon or dimethoate are the ones to use and these will also control some of the other pests such as aphids and thrips. The latter are small insects which suck sap from the foliage and pods leaving them with a silvered appearance. Late sowings are the most likely ones to be affected.

Other pests to watch for are pigeons and mice.

Mildew can be prevalent in dry seasons and adequate watering will do much to prevent occurrences but you will have to resort to fungicides once the disease has a hold.

Failure of the pods to fill can be the result of a number of cultivation deficiencies and you may have to do some detective work to discover which. Cool, showery weather at flowering time may result in a lack of insects to carry out the pollination of the pea flowers. Excessively hot or very dry weather will also cause incomplete pollination. Another factor can be too much nitrogen in the soil which will encourage the growth of the leaves at the expense of the pods, and, later in the season, drought may be a cause.

Peppers

SOW March
HARVEST August
YIELD Varies with type

Peppers can be divided into two groups: the sweet peppers and the chillies or hot peppers. Both types are grown in the same way and are green when young turning to red when fully ripe.

Position These are half-hardy plants which can either be grown throughout in a greenhouse or, in mild areas, can be sown in heat and hardened off for planting out in early June. But, in my opinion, it is really more satisfactory to raise them under glass. If grown out of doors they require a light, fairly rich soil and a sunny sheltered bed. Peppers are not heavy feeders and too much organic matter in the soil will cause over-production of leaves at the expense of the yield.

Cultivation Sow the seeds in March in a warm greenhouse and transplant the seedlings to 3-in. pots. These should either be hardened off for planting outside, 18 in. apart, in early June or potted on into 6-in. pots of John Innes No. 3 compost for growing on in greenhouses.

Subsequent treatment is the same for both methods of cultivation – pinch out the growing points when the plants are 6 in. high and stake them. Feed with liquid manure when the fruits are swelling and keep outdoor crops well hoed and regularly watered.

The peppers should be ready at the end of August and it is important to pick continuously to keep them coming. They can be used at any stage of development and change colour from green to yellow and then red as they ripen.

Varieties Sweet pepper – New Ace and Canapé, both F_1 hybrids, Bull-nosed.

Chilli – Mixed.

What goes wrong Red spider mite and greenfly are the most serious pests but this is a crop which should be relatively free from troubles.

Potatoes

PLANT March (early)
April (mid-season and late)
HARVEST June to July (early)
August onwards (mid-season and late)
YIELD 12 lb. to a 10-ft. row
STORE In a dark, frostproof place

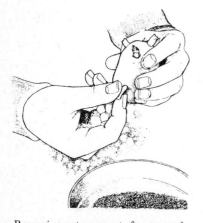

Removing extra sprouts from a seed potato

Potatoes require a lot of valuable space and are subject to a number of diseases so it is not worth growing a main crop unless you have a larger than average garden. However, I do like to grow a few rows of early potatoes as the flavour is better than anything you can buy.

Position A good rich, well-manured and well-dug soil. If possible dress the soil with animal manure in the autumn or winter preceeding planting and also fork in a general fertilizer at about 4 oz. per sq. yd. before planting. On light soils especially plenty of organic matter should be added and it will be necessary to water well in dry weather.

Cultivation Potatoes are grown from tubers known as 'seed' which can be bought as certified free of virus. In January these seed potatoes should be stood in shallow boxes, eye ends uppermost, in a light frostproof place to sprout. Before planting I always rub off all but three of the strongest sprouts on each tuber.

Then in late February or early March plant them in a very sheltered position or in any position if you leave it until the end of March. Plant 15 to 18 in. apart in rows $2\frac{1}{2}$ to 3 ft. apart and cover them with 3 in. of soil. The best way is to take out a V-shaped trench, about 5 in. in depth, and plant in this. Sprinkle a general fertilizer over the surface after planting. When the shoots appear draw some soil over them to provide frost protection and continue this earthing up until the potatoes are growing in ridges.

In mid-April you might consider making a planting of the salad potato Pink Fir Apple. This has long, narrow, pink tubers and makes a very tasty dish, particularly good at Christmas time. Culture is as for other potatoes.

If you do have sufficient space, then plant main crop potatoes in April – again following the previous planting instructions. Spray with Bordeaux mixture or a copper fungicide in early July as a routine prevention against potato blight.

The earlies can be lifted in June or July as soon as they are large enough, this is usually when they are beginning to flower. Main crop potatoes should be lifted in October for storing. Choose a fine day and leave the tubers on the ground for a few hours to dry. Then put all the sound, undamaged tubers in paper or hessian bags and store them in a dark, frostproof place.

Forcing potatoes If you have a greenhouse, I think it is well worthwhile to grow some pots of early potatoes. In a heated greenhouse the sprouted seed can be planted in January but in an unheated greenhouse you should wait until late February or early March. I use a mixture of John Innes No. 3 compost and peat in equal parts and plant five potatoes in a 9- or 10-in. pot or three potatoes in a 7- or 8-in. pot. Half fill the pots and put the potatoes 1½ to 2 in. deep, then, as they grow, topdress with the same potting compost and peat mixture to bring the level to within an inch of the top to allow room for watering. Give plenty of water and keep the pots in a light position. The first potatoes should be ready from a heated greenhouse from about mid-April while those grown in an unheated greenhouse will be ready from May onwards.

Varieties There are a large number of varieties and the choice is very much a matter of personal opinion. A heavy cropping early kind is Arran Pilot but for flavour I prefer Sharpe's Express. Epicure is another useful early kind and all of these are good for growing in pots. Midlothian Early and Home Guard are other early varieties.

Main crop varieties include Pentland Crown, Majestic and King Edward VII.

What goes wrong The potato is subject to attack from a wide range of pests and diseases but these are mostly troublesome with the main crop kinds. Slugs, eelworms and wireworms are the commonly occurring pests and the eelworm is the most serious of these.

Potato blight, scab, wart disease and virus are the diseases to look out for.

As a rule potatoes dislike chalky soils and if grown in these the tubers may be waxy and have little flavour. Home Guard (early) and Majestic (main crop) are both suitable for such soils.

Planting potatoes in a pot to produce an early crop

Pumpkin

SOW May
HARVEST September
YIELD Varies with the individual fruits
STORE In a dry frostproof place

As pumpkins are gross feeders and need a great deal of room they are not practical for the small garden but if space is available then they make a fascinating crop.

Position Pumpkins require rather a lot of space but they will tolerate a partially shady situation. They are grown in a similar manner to marrows and a generous quantity of rotted organic matter is necessary in the soil if large fruits are to be achieved. Dig in well-rotted manure or compost at the rate of a barrowload to each plant.

Cultivation This is a half-hardy plant, so sow the seeds under glass in May and harden off for planting out in early June. Set the plants out at distances of about 6 ft. and then follow the cultural treatment given for marrow. Attention to regular feeding and watering is particularly important. As soon as the pumpkins reach their maximum size reduce watering and stop feeding. They should be allowed to ripen on the plants and harvested in September. Store in a dry frostproof place for winter use.

It is usually sufficient to allow four fruits to develop on each plant but if you want to grow giant specimens then only one or two pumpkins should be left on each plant.

Varieties Hundredweight, Hubbard Squash Golden.

What goes wrong Watch out for slugs, snails and mice.

Radish

SOW February with protection
March to mid-August out of doors
HARVEST April to September
Autumn and winter (winter radish)
YIELD 4 lb. to a 10-ft. row

Types of radish

Radishes are one of the easiest and fastest growing of the root crops and are especially useful as a catch crop between slow-growing vegetables such as celery.

Position Good rich soil is best as radishes need to grow fast if they are to be crisp and mild flavoured. The soil should be topdressed with a general fertilizer before sowing takes place.

Cultivation The seeds are sown thinly in ½-in. deep drills set 5 or 6 in. apart or as a catch crop between celery trenches. To maintain a succession of crops sowings can be made fortnightly from March to mid-August, although unless you can provide a moist shady position during the summer it is very difficult to produce tender radishes from June to August. However, with frame or cloche protection, a sowing can be made in February to give earlier crops.

Hoe regularly and water freely in dry weather so that there is no check to growth.

WINTER RADISH These have large and distinctively flavoured roots which can be sliced for salads. Sow the seeds in July in rows 12 in. apart and thin the seedlings to 8 in. apart. Pull the roots as required and protect them with straw or bracken in very severe weather.

Varieties French Breakfast Forcing (for protected cultivation), French Breakfast, Cherry Belle.

Winter radish – China Rose, Black Spanish.

What goes wrong Radishes belong to the same family as the cabbage and are likely to be affected by the same diseases, see page 45. The worst pest is the flea beetle but birds may do a lot of damage to young plants and in this case the best deterrent is netting or cotton threaded in a zig-zag fashion over the plants.

From the cultivation point of view the most important factor is to keep the radishes growing quickly.

Rhubarb

PLANT March
HARVEST March to July
YIELD Varies with age

Rhubarb is a large leaved perennial which needs a complete growing season before it produces much in the way of edible stalks.

Position Rich, well-cultivated, well-drained soil in a sunny, open position.

Cultivation Plant the divisions or crowns 2 in. below the surface of the soil and 3 ft. apart each way in early spring. Topdress with manure or compost each February, forking it lightly into the soil. Remove all flower stalks directly they appear. The plants should be lifted, divided and replanted every four years in February.

Rhubarb can also be raised from seeds which should be sown in a

Forcing rhubarb

Salsify

sow April and May
HARVEST October
YIELD 6 lb. to a 10-ft. row
STORE In sand or peat in a cool shed

Salsify

Savoy

sow April to May
HARVEST October to March
YIELD 15 lb. to a 10-ft. row

frame in March or out of doors in a seed bed in April. Sow 1 in. deep in rows set 1 ft. apart and thin the seedlings to 6 in. apart. The plants can be moved to their permanent quarters in the autumn.

No stalks should be gathered during the first year to give the crowns time to build up in size. Cropping can begin in the second year and then the young stalks are pulled cleanly away from the crowns – a few at a time from each plant. In order not to weaken plants unduly it is not wise to continue pulling after July. Topdress with a general fertilizer when pulling is finished. Without forcing, harvesting can begin out of doors from about mid-April, but earlier sticks can be obtained by covering the crowns with upturned buckets or boxes in January or February, these being covered in turn with fresh manure and straw or leaves if possible.

To obtain supplies about a month in advance of this, lift some strong roots from November onwards and pack them close together in deep boxes with light soil around them. Place the boxes in a shed or cellar or under the greenhouse staging and make sure that most of the light is excluded by covering the plants with boxes or hanging sacks along the front of the staging. Keep the plants moist and in a temperature of 13 to 24°C. (55 to 75°F.) and sticks should be ready for pulling in three or four weeks. Roots two to five years old are best for this purpose and it is a good idea to expose them to frost for a few days before bringing them inside. Roots which have been forced should be burned as they are not worth replanting.

Varieties Victoria, Holstein, Bloodred.

What goes wrong There should be very little problem from pests or diseases with exception of a rot, crown rot, which may affect leaf stalks and the crowns, eventually destroying them with a soft brown rot. The best control is to lift and burn infected plants.

Salsify is a little known root vegetable which goes by the exotic common name of vegetable oyster – due to its distinctive oyster-like flavour when cooked. It looks like a long thin parsnip.

Position If possible grow in soil that has been manured for a previous crop and well dug. Do not grow them in freshly manured ground – the rule, of course, for all root crops. The soil should be dressed with a general fertilizer at 2 oz. to the sq. yd., before sowing.

Cultivation The seeds are sown in ½-in. deep drills set 15 in. apart and the seedlings are thinned to 9 in. apart. Two sowings can be made, the first in April and the second, to provide roots for winter use, in May.

The roots will be ready for the table in the autumn and can be stored in sand or peat for use when required. Take care when harvesting not to break them.

Varieties Suttons' Giant, Mammoth Sandwich Island.

This is the cabbage that has very hard wrinkled leaves and because it is so hardy it is especially valuable during the winter months. It is grown the same way as the autumn and winter cabbage (page 45). Remember that the ground should be deeply dug and well firmed. There are a number of varieties to cover the period from autumn to spring and those which mature late are especially valuable.

Varieties Best of All (October, November), Early Drumhead (October), Late Drumhead, Ormskirk Late Green (January to March), Rearguard (December to March).

What goes wrong The pests and diseases are the same as for cabbage.

Scorzonera

SOW May
HARVEST September
YIELD 6 lb. to a 10-ft. row
STORE In sand or peat in a cool shed

This is another little known vegetable which is grown for its long black roots which have a particularly delicate flavour.

Position Soil preparation is the same as for parsnips, (page 60).

Cultivation The seeds are sown in May in ½-in. deep drills set 15 in. apart and the resulting seedlings are thinned to 9 in. apart. It is not wise to make a sowing earlier than May as this vegetable has a tendency to run to seed if sown early.

The roots are ready for lifting in late September and can be stored in sand or peat in a cool airy shed.

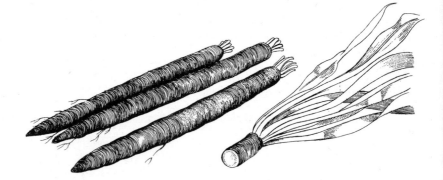

Seakale

PLANT March
HARVEST December to March

Below Making cuttings of seakale *Below right* A trimmed root *Far right* Roots of seakale potted up

This is another vegetable which is a little out of the ordinary and I do suggest that you give it a try. It is grown for the young shoots which must be blanched in darkness.

Position Well-dug and well-manured soil.

Cultivation In March plant 6- to 8-in. long root cuttings (often known as thongs), so that the tops are about ½ in. below the surface of the soil. Make sure they are the right way up – the usual method when making the cuttings is to cut the upper end straight and the lower end slanting to make them easily identifiable – and space them 1½ ft. apart in rows 2 ft. apart.

Keep the plants well hoed and when the young shoots start to grow

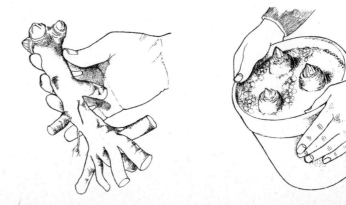

remove the smallest and weakest and leave only one shoot on each root.

The roots will have developed into strong crowns by November when they can be lifted. Trim off the side roots close to the main stem and prepare them as root cuttings as described previously, then tie them in bundles and store them in sand in a sheltered place for planting the following spring. The crowns are also placed in a sheltered place out of doors and covered with sand. At regular intervals pot or box up a few crowns at a time, water well, and bring them into a warm greenhouse (minimum temperature 13°C., 55°F.) or shed to force into growth. Make sure they are kept in complete darkness during forcing – black polythene is an excellent light excluder. The shoots should be ready for cutting in about four or five weeks' time when they are between 6 and 9 in. long.

Seakale can be raised from seeds sown in April out of doors but this method requires two years before seedlings are strong enough to force.

In January the crowns left out of doors can be forced in situ by placing boxes, pots or even soil over them to bring about blanching.

Shallots

PLANT February to March
HARVEST July onwards
YIELD 10 lb. to a 10-ft. row
STORE In a frostproof place and by pickling

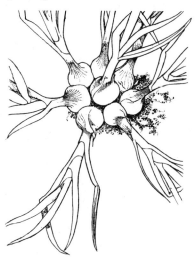

Shallots are easy to grow and make a useful substitute for onions as well as being very good for pickling.

Position A sunny spot and deeply dug and well-drained soil manured for a previous crop. It is important not to make the soil too firm as this encourages the bulbs to push themselves out of the ground.

Cultivation In February or early March, plant the bulbs 6 to 9 in. apart in rows 1 ft. apart and barely cover them with soil. Hoe frequently and in June move some soil away from the bulb clusters to expose them to the light and assist ripening. As soon as the foliage dies down the bulbs should be lifted and laid on the surface, or better still, in a frame to dry for a few days before storing in an airy, cool but frostproof place. Rub away any loose outer skins before putting the shallots in store and keep aside some medium sized healthy bulbs for replanting in spring.

Shallots can also be increased from seed sown thinly in drills 8 in. apart in March.

Varieties Longkeeping Yellow and Jutland Yellow AA Grade.

What goes wrong Shallots are subject to the same range of diseases as the onion. Virus infection can be serious and all suspected bulbs should be pulled out and burned. Plant only healthy bulbs from good stock.

Another problem may be soft rot which can seriously affect bulbs in store if they have not been well ripened and stored in good conditions.

Spinach

SOW March to July (summer)
August to September (winter)
HARVEST May to October (summer)
October to April (winter)
YIELD 3 to 4 lb. to a 10-ft. row

Two kinds of spinach are grown: the summer or round-seeded and the winter or prickly seeded and by sowing both it is possible to maintain a supply throughout the year. This is a fast growing crop which does not take kindly to hot, dry conditions.

Position Well-worked and manured soil with a good lime content in sun or partial shade. Choose a sheltered place for the winter kind. Topdress with a general fertilizer before sowing.

Cultivation Summer spinach should be sown in small quantities once a fortnight from mid-March to mid-July and winter spinach in mid-August or even later in sheltered areas.

Sow the seeds in 1-in. deep drills set 1 ft. apart, and thin gradually to 9 in. (4 in. is sufficient for the winter kind).

As spinach soon runs to seed if allowed to become dry, water well in dry weather. Gather leaves as soon as they are of usable size. In cooler areas, protect the winter spinach with cloches or straw during very cold weather.

Although not a true spinach, the rather succulent New Zealand spinach is a useful choice for hot, dry soils where the ordinary spinach will not grow successfully. It has a rather trailing habit and thick, fleshy leaves. The seed is sown under glass in mid-April or in May out of doors. The seedlings raised under glass should be hardened off for planting out once danger of frost is passed.

Varieties Summer type–Longstanding Round, which does not bolt quickly.

Winter type–Longstanding Prickly.

What goes wrong The main difficulty is to prevent the crop bolting too quickly during hot weather and this tendency will be greatly increased if the plants are suffering from lack of moisture or are starved. Therefore, good soil preparation coupled with plenty of water and frequent hoeing are most important.

Spinach Beet

sow April and August
HARVEST Spring and summer, autumn in mild areas
YIELD 5 lb. to a 10-ft. row

This is a form of beetroot grown for its leaves which are used like spinach. It continues to crop for months and is very hardy.

Position As for beetroot.

Cultivation To maintain a good supply, seed should be sown twice– in early April and in early August–in drills 1 in. deep and 18 in. apart. Thin the young plants to 9 in. and pick the leaves continuously pulling them from the outside of the plants, but be sure to eat them while they are young.

If the autumn is mild, the August sowing will provide leaves for pulling then, although the main production period will be in spring.

For plants growing in rather poor soil, a dressing of a high nitrogen fertilizer at 2 oz. to the sq. yd. will help to promote leaf growth.

Swede

sow May or June
HARVEST October onwards
YIELD 8½ lb. to a 10-ft. row
STORE In a cool airy shed in sand or peat

Swedes or Swedish turnips are a popular root crop particularly useful for storing for winter use. They may be confused with turnips but they are, in fact, larger and have a more distinct neck or stem.

Position Well-dug soil which has been manured for a previous crop. Before sowing topdress with a general fertilizer at 2 oz. to the sq. yd.

Cultivation In May or June, sow the seeds thinly in drills ½ in. deep and 15 in. apart. Thin to 9 in. apart.

Swedes require a lot of moisture so hoe frequently to keep down weeds and water during dry periods. Lift for use from October and store the excess in a cool airy shed. In milder areas the roots can be left in the soil throughout the winter and dug up as required.

Varieties Purple Top, Bronze Top.

What goes wrong Pests and diseases are mostly the same as those attacking turnips. There is, however, one problem–brown heart–which affects swedes far more than it does turnips. The centre of the root develops brownish areas and affected roots are unsuitable for eating. This trouble is more likely to occur in dry seasons on light soils, so good cultivation is important.

Sweet Corn

SOW April with protection
May out of doors
HARVEST Early August to the end
of October
YIELD 10 or more cobs to a 10-ft.
row

This vegetable is a favourite of mine and is gradually becoming more widely grown in this country.

Position Good, well-manured soil and a sunny situation.

Cultivation In late April or early May sow the seeds singly ⅛ in. deep in small pots of seed compost and germinate under glass or in a frame at a temperature of 13°C. (55°F.). The seedlings are hardened off for planting out of doors in late May. Space the plants 15 in. apart in rows 3 ft. apart but make short rows to produce blocks of plants rather than long single rows as this will improve pollination, which is by wind. The pollen is blown from the male tassels at the top of the plants to the silks on the ends of the young cobs.

Alternatively, the seeds can be sown two or three together at a similar spacing and 1 in. deep out of doors in early May, thin the seedlings to leave one at each point.

Water well in dry weather and hoe frequently to keep down weeds. Remove all offshoots from the base of each plant and feed in June with a general fertilizer. Once the tassels wither the cobs should be tested for ripeness – when fit for harvesting the seed should exude a milky juice when punctured with a knife point or fingernail. Pick at once by twisting the ears off.

Varieties John Innes Hybrid, Golden Bantam and the F₁ hybrids such as First of All, Earliking, Early Xtra Sweet.

What goes wrong This is a vegetable which has not yet been extensively grown in Britain and is largely unaffected by pests or diseases.

Sweet corn, showing the tassel-like male flowers at the top of the plant and the cobs near the base

Tomato

SOW March or April (under glass)
HARVEST July to October
YIELD Under glass 10 lb. per plant
Out of doors 4 lb. per plant

Removing a side shoot

Tomatoes can be grown out of doors or under glass and a range of varieties suitable for each method of cultivation is available.

Outdoor cultivation Sow the seeds – 2 to each 3-in. pot in John Innes seed compost or soilless compost – under glass in late March or April and keep in a minimum temperature of 16°C. (60°F.). The seedlings are thinned out to retain the best one in each pot and are removed to a frame in May and hardened off for planting out of doors in early June. Set the plants 1½ ft. apart in rows 2½ ft. apart in well-drained loamy soil containing plenty of rotted manure, compost or peat and choose a sheltered, sunny position, ideally south facing.

With the exception of bush varieties each plant should be kept to a single stem by removing all the side shoots which form in the axils of the leaves with the main stem and the stems must be secured to canes or stakes. Water well in warm weather; a good way of doing this is to sink a 5-in. pot about 6 in. from each plant at the time of planting. The pot can then be filled with water as often as required and the water will seep into the soil, reaching the plants at root level. When four flower trusses have been produced pinch out the main growing point. Continue to water liberally and, in addition, feed the plants regularly with a proprietary tomato fertilizer.

To help the lower trusses to ripen remove some of the foliage, and from the end of September when there is danger of frost at night pick all the fruits as they begin to colour and ripen them indoors in a warm dark place such as an airing cupboard. To hasten ripening at this time of year and to protect the fruits I think it is a good idea to untie the plants from their stakes, lay them on straw on the ground and cover them with cloches.

There are a number of bush varieties which are popular for outdoor cultivation and with these the plants are not restricted to a single stem but are allowed to grow naturally without removal of side shoots. The result is low, well-branched plants which need little or no support. All other aspects of cultivation are as for the single stemmed outdoor varieties.

Greenhouse cultivation For this type of cultivation, I like to sow seeds in mid-March, though this is done in February by some gardeners. For successful germination a temperature of about 16°C. (60°F.) is required and a propagation frame within the greenhouse will come in handy for this. Sow the seed very thinly in pots or boxes filled with seed compost and do not cover them with more than ⅛ in. of soil. Cover the container first with glass and then with a sheet of paper to minimize moisture losses. Germination should take place in about a week and the covering must then be removed. Place the containers on a shelf near the glass to ensure that the seedlings grow sturdily and do not become drawn.

As soon as they can be easily handled pot them singly into 3½-in. pots of John Innes No. 1 compost. When they are about 4 in. high re-pot into 5-in. pots and eventually pot on into 9-in. pots of John Innes No. 3 compost or equivalent good loamy soil. Alternatively, plant in beds of good soil, spacing them 1½ ft. apart in rows 3 ft. apart.

As with outdoor varieties, the side shoots should be removed to restrict growth to one main stem. This is tied to a cane or supported by soft string secured to the rafters or to wire strained beneath the rafters. Pinch out the growing tips when they reach the glass and water the plants moderately at first, increasing the quantity as the plants become established.

On bright days from May onwards spray the plants overhead with water to assist the flowers to set fruit. Do this at midday, and close the ventilators for about half an hour to create a humid atmosphere. Bring the atmospheric conditions gradually back to normal afterwards or outbreaks of fungal diseases will be encouraged. Once the first fruits are set, feed every week with one of the proprietary tomato liquid or dry fertilizers. A minimum temperature of 13°C. (55°F.) should be maintained throughout.

RING CULTURE This is another method of cultivation which has become popular for growing tomatoes both out of doors and under glass. Its main advantages are that only a relatively small amount of soil is needed and that there is less risk of infections, such as verticillium wilt, coming from the soil. With the ring culture method, two roots systems are encouraged to develop – fine feeding roots which are confined to the compost (John Innes No. 3 compost or a soilless tomato compost) in bottomless containers, while the water supply is mainly obtained by other coarser roots which delve into a bed of some sterile aggregate (pea gravel, sand or ashes) below the containers.

Ring culture

The plants are grown to the final potting or planting stage as already described, but are then placed in the special bottomless rings and stood on a 6-in. layer of the chosen aggregate. Water is supplied only to the aggregate after the initial watering in and the compost in the rings is fed once a week with a liquid proprietary tomato fertilizer after the first fruits have formed. In this way, the plants take up only as much water as they want but it is vital that the aggregate bed is kept constantly moist. The plants are trained and stopped as previously described.

TOMATO BAGS Another popular and very simple method of culture is by the peat compost plastic bag system. In this case the bags, which are specially manufactured, are opened and planted with two plants to each bag. After this the plants are grown on as they would be when grown conventionally. This method also provides a good check against wilt.

Varieties Ailsa Craig is my favourite, but Alicante and Eurocross have also done well for me. A good yellow one is Tangella. For outdoor bush tomatoes I would choose The Amateur or French Cross.

What goes wrong Tomatoes may be affected by a formidable number of diseases which include stem rot, potato blight, root-rot, leaf mould, virus and verticillium wilt. In addition, there are such physiological disorders as blossom end rot and blotchy ripening which are caused by cultural faults. Attention to cultivation details will help to keep some of these in check or at least to prevent their spread.

The pests are not so important but watch out for attacks from wireworms, whitefly, red spider mite and eelworm.

Turnips

SOW March to September
HARVEST June onwards
YIELD 8 lb. to a 10-ft. row
STORE In a cool airy shed in sand or peat

Turnips are a root crop which can be produced over a long period if cloches are available to provide protection early in the year.

Position This is a crop which needs to be grown quickly so the soil must be rich, well worked and preferably manured for a previous crop. A good supply of moisture in summer is essential.

Cultivation Sow the seeds in small quantities successively from March to August. The seed bed should be well firmed and the shallow drills set 12 to 15 in. apart. Thin the seedlings to 6 to 9 in. apart. Keep well hoed and watered and feed occasionally with small topdressings of a general fertilizer.

Early crops can be produced in frames or under cloches when sowing can take place in mid-February.

The roots can be pulled when they are a reasonable size. For winter use pull in October, cut the tops off and store in sand or peat in a shed or cellar.

Turnip tops for use as 'greens' in spring are produced by sowing a hardy variety in early September and leaving the seedlings to grow unthinned.

Varieties Early Snowball and Golden Ball.

What goes wrong The main diseases are club root, mildew and soft rot while flea beetle is the most serious pest.

Plants which show a tendency to bolt, that is to run up to seed without producing roots, may have too much nitrogen in the soil. This condition may also be caused by loose soil or by transplanting seedlings.

A Sowing and Harvesting Chart for the Principal Vegetables

■ sowing out of doors ▨ sowing under glass ☐ sowing under cloches □ main harvesting period

	JAN.	FEB.	MAR.	APRIL	MAY	JUNE	JULY	AUG.	SEPT.	OCT.	NOV.	DEC.
BEANS, BROAD		▨	▨ ■■	■■■■	■■■■	■■■■	■■■				■■	
						□□□□	□□□□	□□□□	□□□□	□□		
BEANS, FRENCH		■■	■■■■		□□□□	■■■■	■■■■	■				
							□	□□□□	□□□□	□□□□	□□□	
BEANS, RUNNER			■■■■		■■ ■■							
						□□□□	□□□□	□□□□	□□			
BEETROOT				■■■	■■■■	■■■■	■■					
							□□□□	□□□□	□□□□	□□□□		
BROCCOLI	□□□□	□□□□	□□□□ ■■	■■■■ ■■	□□□□	□□			□□	□□□□	□□□□	□□□□
BRUSSELS SPROUTS	□□□□	□□□□ ▨	■■						□□□□	□□□□	□□□□	□□□□
CABBAGE SUMMER			▨	■■■			□□□	□□□□	□□□□	□□□□		
AUTUMN AND WINTER	□□□□	□□□	■■	■■■■	■■					□□□□	□□□□	□□□□
SPRING		□□□□	□□□□	□□□□	□□□□		■■	■■				
CARROTS			□□□□	■■■■	■■■■	■■						
						□□□	□□□□	□□□□	□□□□	□□□□	□□	
CAULIFLOWER		■■	■■■■	■■■■	■■				■■■	■■		
				□□□□	□□		□□	□□□□	□□□□	□□□□	□□□□	
CELERY	□□□□		▨	■■■■	■■				□□□□	□□□□	□□□□	□□□□
CUCUMBER FRAME	■■■	■■■■	□□□□	□□□□			□□□□	□□□□	□□□□			
RIDGE				■■	■■				□□□□	□□□□	□	
KALE	□□□□	□□□□	□□□□	■■■■	■■						□□□□	□□□□
				□□□□	□□□							
KOHL-RABI				■■	■■■■	■■■■	■■■■	■■				
						□□□□	□□□□	□□□□	□□□□	□□□□		
LEEKS	■■	■■	■■	■					□□□□	□□□□	□□□□	□□□□
	□□□□	□□□□	□□□□	□□□□	□□□□							
LETTUCE	□□□□	■■	■■ ■■	■■■■	■■■■	■■■■	■■■■	■■■■	■■■■	■■		□□
		□□□□	□□□□	□□		□□□□	□□□□	□□□□	□□□□	□□□□		
MARROW				■■	■■				□□□□	□□□□	□□□□	
ONIONS	■■■■		■■■■	■■■■			■■■	■■■	■■■			▨
		□□	□□□□	□□□□	□	□□□	□□□□	□□□□	□□□□	□□		
PARSNIPS	□□□□	□□□□	■■	■■	■■■■	■■				□□□	□□□□	□□□□
									□□□			
PEAS	▨	■■■■	▨	■	■■■■	■■■■	■■■			▨		
						□□□□	□□□□	□□□□				
POTATOES EARLY	■■	■■■■	■■■		□□	□□□□	□□□□	□□□□				
MAIN CROP				■■■					□□□□	□□□□	□□□□	
RADISH	□□□□	■■	■■■■	■■■■	■■■■	■■■■	■■■■	■■				□□□□
		□	□□	□□	□□□□	□□□□	□□□□	□□□□	□□□□	□□	□□□	
SAVOY	□□□□	□□□□	□□□□	■■■	■■■■				□□□□	□□□□	□□□□	
SHALLOTS		■■	■■					□□	□□□□	□□□		
SPINACH	□□□□	□□□□	□□□□ ■■	■■■■	■■■■	■■■■	■	■■■■	■■■			□□□□
			□□□□	□□□□	□□□□	□□□□	□□□□	□□□□	□□□□	□□□□	□□□□	
SPINACH BEET		□□□□	□□□□ ■■					■■	□□□□	□□□	□	
SWEDES	□□□□	□□□□	□		■■■	■■■				□□□□	□□□□	□□□□
TOMATO			▨	■■■■	■■				□□□□	□□□□	□□□	
TURNIPS	□□□□	■■ □□□□	■■ □	■■	■■■■	■■■■	■■■■	■■	■	□□□□	□□□□	□□□□
						□□	□□□□	□□□□	□□□□			
	JAN.	FEB.	MAR.	APRIL	MAY	JUNE	JULY	AUG.	SEPT.	OCT.	NOV.	DEC.

Herbs

The cultivation of herbs is both fascinating and worthwhile as they add a variety of flavours to a wide range of culinary dishes. I think that a few of the herbs are a must for the garden, namely parsley, sage, thyme and mint but if you have the space, there are many others which can be grown with advantage and I have described a selection of these. Of course, there are also the herbs used mainly for their fragrance, and I am thinking here of such plants as chamomile and lavender, but these are outside the scope of this book.

The majority of the herbs are not difficult to grow and they require only a small area of ground. In fact, they can be cultivated very satisfactorily in pots and window boxes. So for people without a garden or with only a small amount of space, a few pots on the window-sill or beside the kitchen door can yield a supply of the most popular herbs for a greater part of the year. One thing I would like to stress is that the herbs should be readily accessible to the kitchen, in fact, the closer the better.

General Cultivation With regard to the basic requirements for good growth, most herbs are well satisfied with the same conditions. If we take into account the fact that many of these plants grow naturally on the cliffs of the Mediterranean regions, it follows that a light, well-drained and rather chalky soil is the ideal medium. As I have already indicated a heavy soil can be improved considerably by deep digging in winter combined with the addition of garden compost or peat. The other almost universal requirement is a warm, sunny and well-sheltered position.

For growing in containers use John Innes No. 1 compost and once again make sure that the pots are standing in a sunny sheltered place. Growing herbs in pots is the best way of overcoming adverse soil conditions.

Aftercare is very simple. Unless unusually dry conditions prevail watering is not necessary. Of course, there are always exceptions to every rule and in this case it is parsley, which needs to be kept reasonably well watered. Keep an eye, too, on pot-grown plants as these are likely to dry out quickly. For the majority of the herbs I would also dispense with feeding as this will only encourage the plants to make a lot of foliage and this can spoil the flavour. Weeding and hoeing, however, are most important both to remove competition for light and air from the weeds and to conserve moisture, so do keep the hoe going between the plants throughout the season. Once the plants are established, the leaves can be cut for use, but be selective about this and take care not to strip the plants.

Propagation There are three ways of increasing herbs. First, by seed. This is used for the annuals and can be done by two methods: either by sowing the seeds out of doors in May in drills $\frac{1}{4}$ to $\frac{1}{2}$ in. deep and 9

Taking a heel cutting

to 12 in. apart or by sowing in seed boxes (page 21) under glass in March. Seedlings raised under glass are pricked out as soon as they are large enough to handle and are hardened off for planting outside in May. A word of warning here, the germination of some seeds may be rather slow, this is especially true of parsley which can take up to 42 days.

The shrubby perennial kinds, such as sage and thyme, can be increased by half-ripe cuttings taken in August or September and over-wintered in a greenhouse or frame. These cuttings should be 3 or 4 in. long and cut below a leaf joint. The lower leaves should be trimmed off. John Innes seed compost makes a suitable rooting medium and the cuttings should be inserted around the edge of the pot. An alternative method is to pull off young growths in April or May with a heel of old wood. This heel should be trimmed and the cuttings inserted as before and placed in a shaded frame.

The third method of increase is by division of root clumps, again a useful way of rejuvenating old straggly plants of sage and thyme. The root clumps are lifted and divided into small pieces, each of which has both a root and a bud or shoot. The actual division can be done either with the hands, or, if the roots are particularly woody, with a sharp knife. The best times of year are in the autumn and spring.

Harvesting for drying The most important factor in harvesting herbs is to choose the correct time and this is when the flavour bearing oils are at their most concentrated – usually when the blossoms have just begun to open.

Choose a dry, still day and handle the plants carefully to avoid bruising them. Remove any discoloured and damaged leaves, tie the stems in bunches and hang upside down in a warm airy place. Alternatively, the herbs can be laid in boxes or trays and covered with muslin to keep the dust off; once again keep them in a warm airy place and turn them frequently. When the leaves are brittle, strip them from the stems and pack in air-tight containers.

Some of the herbs, such as parsley, which have rather soft leaves, do not dry well. They can, however, be easily stored in a deep freezer. Simply cut and clean the leaves, blanch them in boiling water, rinse in cold water, drain and pack in polythene bags.

The following list of herbs includes those which I think are essential and a number of others that have a variety of uses.

Basil, Sweet

This is a half-hardy annual which grows to a height of 2 ft. It does best on light, well-drained soil and in a sunny, sheltered position.

Sow the seeds out of doors in mid-May or in pans or boxes of seed compost in March under glass and germinate at 13 to 15°C. (55 to 60°F.). Prick out the seedlings and harden off for planting outside in late May. Pinch out the growing tips to encourage bushiness.

USES The leaves can be chopped and have a wide range of uses, being particularly good in tomato dishes, soups and omelettes. The flavour is a mild mixture of aniseed and spice.

Chives

These are a perennial herb, closely related to the onion, and growing in ordinary soil and a sunny position. Sow the seeds in March in ½-in. deep drills, 6 in. apart and thin the seedlings to 6 in. apart in the rows.

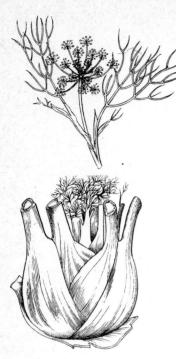

Fennel

Garlic

Chives require very little attention other than hoeing, ample watering in dry spells and a topdressing of compost in early spring. The top growth dies down completely in winter and new leaves are produced from early May, or earlier if the clumps are protected with cloches during the winter.

Every three or four years the plants should be lifted, divided and replanted in February, March or early April. Dig some well-rotted manure into the soil before replanting.

Chives are an excellent crop for growing in window boxes or large pots where they can be readily at hand for kitchen use. A clump or so lifted in September and potted up in John Innes No. 1 compost can be kept indoors to provide leaves during the winter.

USES The fresh leaves have a mild onion flavour and are very useful in salads, soups, sauces and in cheese and egg dishes.

Fennel

A hardy perennial which grows to a height of about 6 ft. It has attractive grey-blue leaves and yellow flowers in July and is a good plant for the back of a flower border.

Fennel grows best in a sunny position and can be easily increased by seeds sown out of doors in late March. It can also be increased by divisions in spring but these are often slow to become established.

USES The leaves can be used to flavour sauces for fish dishes and also in soup. The swollen stem bases can be used as a vegetable.

Garlic

A member of the onion family, garlic is grown for its bulbs each of which is composed of a number of cloves. It likes well-drained soil and an open sunny position.

In March, plant the cloves 2 in. deep and 6 in. apart in rows 12 in. apart. Hoe regularly, but no further attention is needed until July or August when the foliage turns yellow and this indicates that the bulbs are ready for lifting. Lay the bulbs in a sunny place for a few days to dry off before storing in a cool airy shed. They may be tied in small bunches and suspended from a nail or beam.

USES The crushed cloves have a strong and distinctive flavour and are extensively used in a variety of culinary dishes.

Marjoram

There are two kinds – the sweet marjoram and the pot marjoram. Sweet marjoram is a half-hardy annual sown in March in a greenhouse and treated as for basil. It also grows to about 2 ft. high.

Pot marjoram is a hardy perennial which can be grown from seeds sown under glass in March or outside in late April. The old plants can be lifted and divided as necessary.

USES Both kinds have sweet spicy leaves which are good in soups, stews and stuffings.

Mint

Although this is one of the most popular herbs, it can be invasive and will take over the garden if not checked. It is a perennial which spreads by means of runners and I like to plant the runners in a bucket or old tin bath which has been sunk in the soil as this will effectively confine the roots to a definite area.

There are several species but the most commonly grown for the kitchen is the garden mint or spearmint, *Mentha viridis*. Apple mint, *M. rotundifolia*, is also a good choice – excellent for mint sauce.

Mint will grow in full sun or partial shade and is best in a moisture-retentive soil. Plant divisions or runners 9 in. apart in February or early March. Further increase is by division in autumn or spring and by cuttings taken in April or May. It is advisable to make a new bed from young shoots every two years as this helps to prevent the occurrence of mint rust disease.

USES These are almost too well known to list, the leaves being used in cooking, making sauces, jellies and drinks.

Parsley

One of the best-known perennial herbs but usually grown as an annual or biennial. Parsley grows to a height of 1 to 2 ft., and is best in a moderately rich, well-dug soil and an open position. To maintain a year-round supply three sowings should be made annually, one in early March, the second about the end of May and the third in August. Sow the seeds in drills $\frac{1}{4}$ in. deep and 1 ft. apart. Parsley also grows successfully in pots or as an edging to a bed. Thin the seedlings to 9 in. and harvest the leaves a few at a time so that the plants are not weakened. Remove any flower heads which appear.

Some seedlings from the August sowing can be transferred to a frame in October for winter use, alternatively plants may be covered with cloches.

USES Parsley is probably the most commonly grown and popular herb. It is widely used in sauces.

Parsley

Oregano

A hardy perennial with a spreading habit and growing eventually to a height of $2\frac{1}{2}$ ft. It has no special cultural requirements but should be kept trimmed and replanted every three years. Increase by cuttings of young growths.

USES The oval leaves have a slightly bitter flavour and are used with salads, pork dishes and tomatoes.

Rosemary

This is a small ornamental evergreen shrub growing from 3 to 5 ft. high. Rosemary appreciates well-drained soil and a sunny, sheltered position. Increase by cuttings in August or by sowing seeds in April.

USES The grey-green, needle-like leaves have a pungent piny flavour and are excellent with lamb.

Sage

This is a shrubby perennial with grey-green leaves growing to a height of about 2 ft. It likes a sunny place and light, well-drained soil. Cut back after flowering. In cold areas the tops may be damaged by frost in winter and if this happens, cut the bushes back to within 9 in. of the ground. Plenty of young shoots will then grow from the base. In fact, to ensure a good supply of young shoots, all established bushes will benefit from this treatment.

As sage is inclined to become straggly, divide every 3 to 4 years in late February. It can be increased by cuttings in August or September,

Sage

and by seed, which should be sown in March in a cold frame to be planted out when the pots are full of roots.

USES The leaves have an aromatic, slightly bitter tang and are widely used accompanied by onion in stuffings.

Savory

The summer savory is a hardy annual, 9 to 12 in. in height with very fragrant, strongly aromatic leaves. It requires the usual conditions and can be grown from seeds sown out of doors in April.

USES The leaves are somewhat bitter tasting and are used in salads, soups and egg dishes.

Tarragon

A 2-ft. perennial which can be increased by division in spring. Good, well-drained soil is essential and it is advisable to protect the plants with straw or bracken in the winter.

USES The leaves have a flavour reminiscent of liquorice and aniseed and are used in sauces and soups.

Thyme

This is an easy and much appreciated perennial which grows to a height of between 8 and 12 in. It particularly likes a hot dry position and will only flourish in sun and light sandy soil. It tends to get rather straggly and should be replanted every 3 years. Alternatively cut back to about 3 in. above ground level in spring.

Sow seeds in March in pots under glass or outside in April or take tip cuttings in May or June, alternatively, divide in March or April.

USES The pungent leaves are good in stuffings, soups and with fish.

Tarragon

Index